A CHURCH WITHOUT PRIESTS?

A CHURCH WITHOUT PRIESTS?

Jacques Duquesne

Translated from the French
by Bernard Murchland

THE MACMILLAN COMPANY

253
D946c

Contents

Introduction

THERE USED to be a great deal of talk about the "leakage" of
the laity from the Catholic Church. Sparse research on the
subject suggested that about 30 percent of the infants baptized in urban parishes eventually grew up to be dormant
parishioners, or lapsed Catholics, in the sense that they
hardly ever went near a church building. The input, however, by infant and adult baptisms was always so much
greater than the exodus that no one ever talked about a
"Church without laity."

During those years of worry about lay leakage the numbers of the clergy continually increased even to the point
where we were able to send missionary priests to foreign
countries. While it was said that we never really have enough
priests, there was no genuine vocation shortage. Bigger and
better seminaries were being built. Priests were priests forever. When an ordination class celebrated its silver jubilee,
only about 4 percent of them, according to the best statistics
available, had left the ranks of the priesthood, and they were
labeled either sick or sinful. Unlike the Protestant minister
who can move with relative ease into a second career, the defrocked priest was a scandal to men and angels.

Now all this has changed. Suddenly and swiftly the Catholic priesthood has taken on a look of impermanence. In a
recent survey of lower-echelon diocesan clergy almost two-

6

thirds of them agreed that there should be some form of voluntary resignation, of honorable discharge, from the priesthood. The idea of a temporary commitment, instead of a lifelong dedication, seems to have become popular. Minor seminaries are being shut down, and major seminaries are moving to the university campus or are consolidating with others. A frantic re-examination of training procedures is under way and some realistic questions are finally being asked about the professional role of the clergy. Will the proportion of resignations equal, and then gradually exceed, the proportion of newly ordained until we face the prospect of a "Church without priests?"

This is the kind of question that is provocative of a discussion or a debate, rather than evocative of an answer or a solution. Every large-scale organization, if it is to maintain itself in existence and perform its central functions, has to have a cadre of full-time, trained functionaries. To suggest that the Church will remain while its clergy vanishes is to suggest that a university, or a state government, or an industrial system will continue to function without functionaries. A realistic approach to this question involves not the extinction of the priesthood, but the quality and quantity of clergy, the adaptation of their roles, the renewal of the structures within which they operate. As far as the Catholic clergy are concerned, this is what the *aggiornamento* is all about.

Everyone knows that the Second Vatican Council dealt with the ministry and life of priests, with priestly formation, and even with the ministry and life of bishops (who are said to enjoy the "fullness" of the priesthood). Some people felt that the Council was a new dawn for the Church, the beginning of a genuine renovation that would accelerate in subsequent years. They have been disappointed. Others felt that the Council was a temporary nuisance that should be quickly forgotten so that the Church could continue as an island fortress in a sea of instability. They, too, have been disappointed.

The sad fact is that neither the venerable fathers of the Council nor the horde of commentators on the Council documents have provided an intelligent explanation of, or a positive escape from, the so-called "clergy crisis." They have simply milled around within the small circle of sacerdotal reductionism. All they have said, in essence, is that the clergy should learn to perform better the narrowly defined functions of teaching, sanctifying and administering. Certainly this constitutes a recommendation for personal renewal and institutional reform but without leading us out of the blind alley of role conflict and identity crisis.

Actually there are two blind alleys in which the unending discussion of the Catholic priesthood takes place. One is the status differential between the laity and the clergy, which insists that ordained priests should do only that which unordained lay persons cannot do. The other is the notion that the work of the priesthood must be circumscribed by the work of the episcopacy because the priest merely "shares" in a priesthood which only the bishop has in its "fullness."

The distinction of ontic status between laity and clergy, and between priest and bishop, is harmless enough and no one should quarrel with it unless it interferes with function or rigidifies structure. It has done both, and therein lies the problem. It is true, as we all believe, that the sacrament of holy orders makes a difference in a person, but so do the sacraments of baptism and confirmation. Each of these sacraments sets a man apart status-wise from those who have not received them. Social stratification among the people of God may help to specify function, but it should not limit the ministry of service that each owes to all others.

The tension and turmoil among the contemporary clergy

are symptomatic of their dissatisfaction with the system in which they operate. This source of dissatisfaction was delved for me when I asked a group of married priests whether they would come back to the active ministry if they could bring their wives with them. Their response demonstrated that clerical celibacy was by no means the central issue with them. The conditions under which they would re-enter embraced a thorough overhaul of the ecclesiastical system: professional methods of appointments and reassignments, mature communication between subordinates and superiors, opportunities for parochial experimentation, methods of recognition and promotion, representation in policy formation and decision-making.

The reforms asked for center around intelligent, modern, organizational methods. These sources of dissatisfaction are quite different from the reasons often given by Church officials in the past. The quick and easy explanations were that the defector or dissident priest had lost his zeal and stopped praying, or had never genuinely absorbed his excellent seminary training, or—in some rare instances—that he had not been properly "screened" before acceptance into the seminary or ordination to the priesthood. Until recently there seemed to be little recognition that authoritarian mismanagement could kill zeal, demoralize character and frustrate personalities.

It would be an error, of course, to lay the whole clergy crisis at the door of untrained and unperceptive Church officials. Given the human condition and the variety of personality, one can find ineptitude and sloth, immaturity and irresponsibility, among subordinates as well as among superiors. What seems now to be a relatively "new" factor in the current resignation of Catholic priests is the high quality of some of the men who are leaving the priesthood. Often they are men who have had excellent training, were performing well in work that gave them satisfaction, and had good human relationships with their superiors and colleagues as well as with the people they served. They are successfully holding responsible positions in the nonecclesiastical world and they live as exemplary Catholic laymen.

The unexpected departure of this type of man from the priesthood appears to imply a double motivation. The first is an expressed desire for self-fullfilment, to be one's own man, to take more immediate charge of life's activity, with all the risk and uncertainty that such a move entails. The second is a conviction that opportunities for service to mankind are more frequent and effective outside the institutionalized priesthood. There is no reason to jump to the immediate conclusion that these are deceptive rationalizations, and it is too soon to test the extent to which they have been realized.

We need not fear for the survival of the Church and the priesthood, nor should we mourn that a different Church is emerging with a different priesthood. The price of inexorable change is the difficulty we experience in attempting to foresee both its nature and its direction. The most unrealistic, and perhaps un-Christlike, attitude is that which says "good riddance" to former priests. The notion that the Catholic Church should be purified by the resignation or excommunication of all dissidents is likely to eventuate in ecclesiastical suicide: a nonexistent Church with neither clergy nor laity.

JOSEPH H. FICHTER, S.J.
Harvard University
The Divinity School

A *Pastor Commits Suicide*

IN THE QUIET of the evening he made his decision. He
climbed to the attic of the rectory and tied the rope to a
rafter. He thought of his birds, the only creatures in the
world he loved. He did not want them to be dependent on
the good or bad will of anyone, so he opened the cage door
and gave them their freedom. They flew away, without understanding. Then, irrevocably alone in this world, he returned to the attic, secured the rope and, anxious to be with
the God to whose service he had dedicated his life in more
hopeful days, hanged himself.

The chancery, to be sure, did everything possible to hush
up the scandal. The press was discreet as were civil officials.
The bishop's office knew exactly what to do when a priest
called attention to himself in an unexpected or inopportune
manner.

The people of the village respected this discretion. They
were not a very impressive lot, these few hundred peasants,
workers, domestics, children and old people. It was as though
they felt vaguely guilty, a little responsible for the death of
their pastor.

Their pastor? I am not sure that the word is an apt one.
One would have only to visit the church to understand. It
was a sturdy little building of gray stone in the center of the
village, bordered with a patch of lawn where sheep grazed

when the pastures dried up in the summer heat. To the left of the entrance, between two large fir trees, was a replica of Calvary—the gift, no doubt, or a rich landowner in the last century. Or perhaps a former pastor, knowing what to do to obtain money from these ignorant peasants, succeeded in getting them to buy it for the parish in gratitude for some special protection. It had in its day been a fine Calvary but time had begun to take its toll. The crucifix had rotted away at the base. The bronze Christ, which had once been painted silver, had fallen head first into the shrubbery, giving the impression that he had been crucified upside down.

The church was somber, cold and sad. I know nothing sadder than those little country churches with fading banners, vestiges of ancient processions, and their general air of desuetude. The altar was badly covered with a yellow cloth and resembled less a banquet table than the headstone of an abandoned cemetery. This church was like a house of the dead. It is understandable that children who were forced to attend it when they were young had no desire to return. Outside there is the sky, cars, song, television and life. Moreover, the church could barely accommodate sixty persons. Perhaps eighty on special occasions. I counted the benches carefully. It would seem that there had never been many Christians in this parish.

One day, a mild-mannered and well-manicured priest of the type still found in the calm and quiet chancery offices decided to send our pastor here. Nothing could have been simpler: a name matched a vacancy. "Leave as soon as possible," the official letter read. "You are responsible to God and the bishop for this village and its inhabitants. You know what to do. You were well trained in the seminary. Good luck. And do not forget to make an annual financial report so our books can be kept up to date."

Do I exaggerate? Would that I did! But I write the truth. This priest is dead. He committed suicide. And in the heart of France. A priest of that post-conciliar Church that is quite satisfied with itself, despite its pretensions to the contrary, and looks smugly in the mirror to find evidence that it has managed its updating rather well. The pastor I refer to did not live in an inaccessible mountain village. A national highway passed by his church. There was a bus twice a day linking two important cities which were also episcopal sees. The county seat, where the dean resided, was a mere ten miles away. There was a post office and telephone service.

But none of this was of any avail because the pastor died of loneliness. A few women, some children and two or three distracted men constituted his Sunday congregation. There was no one to talk to. The pastor kept his own house because he could not afford a housekeeper. He did not like to cook—although some country pastors do and this helps them kill the time—so he made a large pot of stew at the beginning of the week and reheated a portion of it each day. A farmer's wife, taking pity on his poverty, left him a pint of milk each day, depositing it anonymously on the doorstep in the early morning. Why he didn't go for the milk himself I do not know. Perhaps he felt no one wanted to see him. Moreover, when the government raised the price of milk, this charity ceased, no doubt because it had become ruinously expensive.

He could also have gone of a Sunday afternoon to the local cafe, across the street from the town hall, where the men gathered to play cards. But he did not. It is not easy to mingle with men when one's body is shrouded in a long black soutane, when one is eyed suspiciously as conversation falls off and hostile eyes make it clear that you are an embarrassment to everyone.

Perhaps the pastor was not cut out for this kind of apostolate. Then why had he been sent to this place? And why, when it became clear that he was unhappy, wasn't something done to find him a more congenial position?

He was perhaps not "typical," as they say, of the modern country pastor. Or at least not all of them, since there are all kinds. But he existed. And anyway loneliness is an affliction that besets many different types of country pastors— even the most "modern" who band together like shock troops, ride about in cars and seem literally bursting with dynamism.

Perhaps he was what psychologists call a "depressive." There was no doubt that he was ill. Ulcers in his back were so painful that he had to get up in the night and walk the streets of the village. Then, at least, he was protected from curious eyes. Night spared him the exhausting impression of being spied upon. Still, some unexpected encounters were unavoidable: young people returning from a party in a neighboring village, a father seeking the doctor for a sick child. The villagers knew that he walked at night. "Our pastor is an odd one," said the pious folk of the parish. Others suspected some clandestine adventure.

If a child, an old person, or even a dog lived alone as unhappily as their pastor, the villagers would have called for help. But they did nothing for their priest. They knew nothing about him. He was a perfect stranger, the emissary of another world, a kind of functionary of the sacred, the mechanic of souls, with whom one had dealings only at the time of birth, marriage and death. The rest of the time people preferred to avoid him.

His own family lived in another diocese. He preferred it that way since he had no desire to see them. "I do not want them to know what I have become," he confessed one day. When a son tells his peasant parents that he wants to become a priest, they are not always enthusiastic. But they are consoled by the thought that he will become someone important. At least this is what they thought twenty years ago. What a deception, what a humiliation it would be for them if they knew! Because he loved them he preferred to remain silent. Perhaps he was wrong. He sought solitude to conceal his misery as much as anything else.

Some would say that he was lazy. He could have earned some money by manual labor. This is not an unknown activity among country pastors in France. He had thought about it. He had once raised bees, that traditional escape for French country pastors, and sold some honey, but it hadn't been a great commercial success. He might also have found employment on local farms, although it would not have been easy in that part of the country. The priest "has his place." People don't like sudden reversals of roles. It was all very well for the village to have a pastor, but it he went to work like everyone else, it wouldn't be quite the same and the order of things would be upset.

The dean of the diocese lived nearby, and not a great distance away was the bishop's residence. At the time of the death the bishop was at the Council in Rome. But the diocesan functionaries were there. Didn't they know anything? What did they do? I did not have the courage to make inquiries of them. Perhaps I should have. They no doubt had their reasons, and even good reasons: we are overburdened with administrative work; quite frankly, my dear fellow, we always thought he was unbalanced; he shouldn't have been ordained but, as you know, seminary directors in the past weren't too discriminating; we needed priests; how could we know anything was wrong; he never confided in anyone.

To be sure. But the pastor committed suicide. Those who appointed him and especially those responsible for leaving him there, those who didn't know, didn't see and didn't want to see, must take some of the responsibility. Some of it. But

not all of it. It would be too easy to blame the bishop and let
it go at that. But what if responsibility were more widely
shared? What if the priest's situation in the Church and in
the world conformed to the ideal described by Vatican II?

Others in similar circumstances leave the priesthood. Some
slam the door after them and create a furor. Others, more
discreet, obtain the necessary permissions and dispensations.
They do everything according to the book. Why do they
leave? And why do fervent and committed young Catholics
refuse to enter? Why are so many leaving the seminary before ordination, hesitant?

Cardinal Richaud wrote recently: "We expect much from
the Council and we have every reason to. But I tell you that
the Council will have been in vain if there are not more
priests." Cardinal Richaud's uneasiness is amply justified.
The statistics are convincing: the number of priests is decreasing at a steady rate.

In France between 1870 and 1900 there were 1,500 priests
ordained every year. Between 1930 and 1940 there were
about 1,000. Since 1960 the number of ordinations has
ranged from 500 to 550. Each year the deceased and departures number around 800 in the secular clergy. Thus
since 1961 the Church in France has been losing from 250
to 300 priests annually, enough to staff a small diocese. Nor
is the outlook for the future encouraging. Because many
priests are old (10,000 out of a total of 41,000 were over sixty
years old in 1965; the figure will be 13,000 in 1975) the number of deaths will augment this loss considerably.

Furthermore, ordinations are falling off. From 1963 to 1966
the number of major seminarians has dropped from 5,279
to 4,536. In addition, 400 of these leave the seminary each
year—about half to enter religious orders, the other half to
return to lay life.

There was, until recently, great hope for the minor seminaries. In 1960 there were 16,060 students enrolled in these institutions. But since 1961 there has been a falling off here as well—a loss of some 1,700 students in five years. It is estimated that the number of minor seminarians entering the major seminary will decrease by 10 percent after 1968 and by more than 20 percent after 1970. The statistics for religious orders are about the same, although in some cases worse. Father Leclercq, an oblate of Mary Immaculate, has observed that 70 percent of the young men who enroll in the minor seminaries of his order are not ordained, although every effort is made to keep them.[1] There is one priest per ten students in these seminaries! This may be considered a minimal departure rate since in many congregations it goes as high as 85 percent. At one time there was also great hope for "late vocations." But their numbers have also steadily decreased. Special seminaries for late vocations counted less than 500 aspirants in November, 1966, against 700 for the preceding year.

This is the general situation throughout Europe.

In Belgium seminary enrollment decreased by 35 percent between 1947 and 1965. The number of ordinations in the regular clergy decreased by 15 percent between 1960 and 1967.

In the Netherlands the average number of ordinations between 1947 and 1957 was 357 per annum. There were 279 in 1963. The present ferment in these countries has contributed further to the decline in vocations. As early as 1963 more than half of the major seminarians left before ordination.

In "Catholic" Spain enrollment in minor seminaries has decreased 30 percent since 1958. There is a relatively stable average of ordinations in Italy although 50 percent of the

[1] M. Leclercq, O.M.I., "Un examen de conscience," in *la Vocation* (Paris, Editions du Cerf, 1965).

major seminarians leave before ordination. Between 1850 and 1950 the number of diocesan priests in Italy decreased by two-thirds while in Spain it decreased by one-half (although it is true that some died violently during the Spanish Civil War).

In Germany statistics for major seminaries show a decrease of 10 percent between 1951 and 1965. The percentage of departures among theology students has risen to 40 percent. In Munich in 1964 the number of ordinations was barely one-third of the average number before the war. The situation in Austria is very much the same.

Ireland, where the number of vocations is extraordinarily high (many of them migrate to the United States), is showing the first signs of crisis. It is estimated that the attrition rate in major seminaries between 1961 and 1967 has risen from 35 percent to 50 percent.

What about Latin America? That vast continent numbers 33 percent of the world's Catholics but only 6 percent of its priests. It would require 125,000 vocations to assure the people of one priest per 5,000 faithful (in France there is one priest for 1,300 inhabitants; in Belgium one for 355). There are now about 25,000 priests in Latin America. In Chile 60 percent of the clergy is of foreign origin and 40 percent is over fifty years old. Since 1900 the population of the country has nearly doubled but vocations have for the same period decreased by one-half. In Brazil some 60 million faithful have no contact with a priest. In the villages of Central American countries like Honduras (where there are 200 priests per two million Catholics) experimental programs have been adopted. For example, laymen lead the peasants in a form of common prayer that resembles the Mass. Of course, France, Spain (there are some 30,000 Spanish missionaries in the world), Canada and the United States continue to send priests to Latin America. Is this a good solution? Not necessarily if we are to believe Monsignor Ivan Illich, a somewhat nonconformist American priest who founded a missionary training center in Cuernavaca, Mexico. "Men and money sent with missionary motivation," he wrote for the Jesuit weekly *America*, "carry a foreign Christian image, a foreign pastoral approach and a foreign political message. They also bear the mark of North American capitalism of the 1950's. . . . This kind of foreign generosity has enticed the Latin American Church into becoming a satellite to North Atlantic cultural phenomenon and policy." [2]

In the United States, unlike the situation in most industrialized countries, sacerdotal recruitment is in a healthy state. There were 17,491 priests in 1912 and 55,581 in 1962. In this country everything connected with the religious role has high social prestige. But here, too, the first signs of a crisis are appearing.[3] The same may be said of Canada.

The clergy in Africa is unevenly distributed: 15,660 priests for 360 million inhabitants. The native clergy has increased rapidly. There were 94 African priests in 1922 and more than 2,521 in 1963. But at least twice as many are needed immediately. In 1957, Pius XII addressed the encyclical *Donum Fidei* to the bishops of Europe, urgently appealing to them to send more priests to the Church in Africa. Of 41,000 French priests, 249 went to Africa, although generally on a temporary basis.

"Tomorrow, a Church without priests?" This question is not to be taken lightly. Nor is it intended as a catchy title. The statistics quoted above indicate that a considerable decrease in the number of priests may be the reality of tomorrow throughout the world. It is already the case in many countries today.

The statistics we have cited and the country pastor's sui-

[2] *America*, January 21, 1967, p. 88.
[3] See Chapter 3.

cide have the same meaning: the situation of the man-priest,
both in the Church and in the world, is less and less acceptable. We are aware, of course, of the importance of the crisis
of faith. This is one of the classic reasons why priests leave.
But we are now confronted with something new: most of
the priests who leave the ministry today remain fervent
Christians. Vocations are not only decreasing as such; they
are decreasing as the Catholic population grows. The crisis
of faith cannot explain such a phenomenon.

It is the status of the priest that is questioned. Not the
priesthood as such but the way in which it is lived con-
cretely. Many think that the present structure of the priesthood corresponds neither to the realities nor the possibilities
nor the necessities of the contemporary situation. And there
are fewer and fewer happy priests. As a result, the young
instinctively reject their way of life. Some priests leave. The
majority of them are of the opinion that it is by remaining in
the place they have chosen in the Church that they can best
express their deep commitment. But many spend years fabri-
cating a plate of armor that will protect them against bore-
dom, failure, loneliness and uncertainty.

"No generalization is entirely true, including this one,"
Disraeli is reported to have said. Fortunately there are happy
priests. One of them wondered one day if he was normal
since he felt very much at home while everyone around him
was talking about the "problems" of priests or the crisis in
the clergy. The purpose of this book is to analyze the crisis.
Thus it will say little about happy priests. But I would ask
the reader not to forget that they do exist.

Biblio, a catalogue of books published in French throughout the world, reports that ninety-two books on the crisis in
the priesthood were published between 1960 and 1966. The
real figure is probably higher still. I myself wrote one of

these books.[4] The reason why I make bold to add yet another title to an already long list is because those who confided in me after my first book was published and the contacts I have been afforded with many priests in diverse situations have convinced me that the crisis is getting worse.

Some religious publications give the impression that the conciliar documents have already been magically translated into practice, that the *aggiornamento* fostered by the Council is proceeding apace and that all our problems will soon be solved. This is not the case and informed persons are well aware of this. Canon Aubert, a professor in the University of Louvain, opines that "the Council was a miracle in relation to the past but mere child's play in relation to the future."[5] The present is our business.

The gravity of this crisis disturbs the authorities. On September 9, 1966, Pope Paul VI wrote: "No one can be unaware that a wave of doubt, malaise and uneasiness today besets many priests."[6] Perhaps this wave is stronger than Roman officials realize. When a difficulty is recognized by ecclesiastical authority, it has usually long troubled souls and done much harm (given the "screens" that separate authority from the faithful). Thus it is imperative that we speak about this crisis. First of all for those priests who, either because they are ashamed of their unhappiness or out of respect for ecclesiastical discipline, remain silent. Secondly, for the laity, "members of the people of God" as the Council reminded us, who have the right to be informed about what is going on. We cannot isolate the priest from the people of God. It is, therefore, normal that the laity feel concerned by the problems of the clergy. It is even desirable that they become

[4] *Les Prêtres* (Paris, Grasset, 1965).
[5] *Informations catholiques internationales*, October 15, 1965.
[6] Letter to an Italian study week on pastoral *aggiornamento*.

more concerned than they are. After all, it is the laity who are asked to furnish future priests.

In order to understand the reasons for this wave of doubt, malaise and uneasiness, I think it would be useful first of all to analyze those who leave (either the Church or only the priesthood), their problems and their reasons. These represent an extreme case. But extreme cases are always significant. Economists base much of their theory on "marginal" enterprises which are on the outer fringes of relatively homogeneous activities. What is diffuse and uncertain and sometimes difficult to discern within the normal range is magnified and revealing on the margin. The priest who is on "the outer fringe"—sometimes so much so that he is forced to change his status—can therefore teach us much about those who are not. Each reader can draw upon his personal experience to enlarge the field of investigation or furnish the necessary correctives and nuances. We hope by thus projecting a kind of floodlight on the general situation that no detail will be left in the shadows.

It is not easy to project such a light. Pope Paul VI has appealed to the laity "to feel responsible for the virtue of their brothers who are charged with the mission of serving them in the priesthood for their salvation." [7] This at least supposes that the laity are informed. But those who try to investigate in some detail the problem of priests who leave the clergy meet with the objection from ecclesiastical authorities that it is not opportune to divulge information on this subject. Similarly, the laity are told that they must feel responsible for the financial life of the Church—and that is normal. But those who try to gain some knowledge of the bookkeeping come up against a wall of silence, with rare exceptions. Despite certain efforts that assume the contrary, the Church is not a house of glass.

[7] *Sacerdotalis Caelibatus,* No. 96.

I realize that a problem like this can be painful, particularly for the hierarchical Church. As a member of the Church, I share this suffering. But try as I will I cannot understand why a veil is modestly drawn over this problem. Jacques Maritain once remarked that to many older Christians any admission of failure is "somehow indecent." One might say, he added, "that they fear embarrassing apologies." [8] But they would embarrass the Church much more by letting uninformed imaginations fabricate fictions.

Thus I have questioned a number of priests who left. Not a great number because many of them prefer to remain silent. I have likewise interrogated those who knew them, those who knew their reasons and can—sometimes but not always—distinguish between real reasons and rationalizations. I take this occasion to thank all of them. What they have told me and the results of my research and diverse inquiries conducted on a worldwide basis will serve as the basis for the first part of this book. I shall try at the same time to enlarge the field of vision and raise some broader questions concerning the man-priest. It will then be possible to make some suggestions. Not all of them will be new or original but they seem to correspond to the aspirations of a growing number of priests and perhaps to the needs of the world and the Church.

At a conference of European bishops in Noordwijk (Holland) in July, 1967, Bishop Elchinger of Strasbourg stated that today we must "learn how to take risks in the Church and learn how to listen to what the laity have to say."

That is why I am writing this book.

[8] Cited by Cardinal Leger in an address given in Montreal, April 12, 1966.

PART ONE

Those Who Leave

1

A Theologian Marries

"ON SUNDAY, three weeks before Christmas, I got up from my desk and went to the chapel. I knew that the end of my struggle had come. I intended to leave the Roman Catholic Church."

The man who wrote these accusing words on a December evening in England was the theologian Charles Davis, a forty-three-year-old priest of medium height and somewhat sad demeanor. These lines began his sensational article which appeared in the London *Observer* on January 1, 1967. In it Charles Davis explained the reasons for his decision.

He chose to leave in a cloud of publicity. First of all because he was Charles Davis, England's greatest theologian. His enemies—he like everyone else had them—contested his theological reputation. He was instead an "able popularizer," they said. In any case he was very well known. He had taught philosophy at Heythrope College and for sixteen years at St. Edmund's College. His books were best-sellers and had been translated into many languages. His many lecture tours in the United States were highly successful. He enjoyed, it was said, a great influence. Since 1960 he had been editor in chief of *The Clergy Review*, an edifying and somewhat dull monthly which he tried to update. Beginning with his editorial "Month by Month" in 1964, he engaged in discreet controversy with the traditionalists, and even some laymen began to read the journal. He was a member of the editorial committee of *Concilium,* launched after Vatican II by some of the best theologians who had attended it. Davis himself was John Cardinal Heenan's theological adviser at the Council.

His decision provoked considerable controversy among English Catholics. His stature in that country was comparable to a Congar or de Lubac in France, a Schillebeeckt in Holland or a Karl Rahner of Hans Küng in Germany. His departure sparked diverse reactions: sharp criticism from some, more or less open approval from others. The Dominican Herbert McCabe, editor of *New Blackfriars,* was relieved of his post and placed under ecclesiastical suspension because in commenting on the Davis affair he accused the Roman Church of being "corrupt." He submitted to the sanctions—the suspension was lifted eight days later—but the English Catholic press was enraged because he was condemned without having been given a chance either to explain or to retract his position. Dr. John Bryden, the president of the Newman Association, went to Rome to submit a protest signed by 850 laymen to the master general of the Dominicans. The association asked English Catholics to fast on March 11, "in reparation for the sins against justice and charity committed within the Roman Catholic Church for which we are all responsible."

The archbishop of Birmingham consecrated a pastoral letter to the Davis case. He called for calm and trust. "What happened has often happened in the history of the Church, especially after great Councils such as the one just held." Cardinal Heenan declared: "Charles Davis' conscience and personal relations are his affair. Now the best means we have to show our friendship is to pray that God will guide him in all that he undertakes."

In a word, the Davis affair created an uproar—the more
so because English Catholics are not used to this kind of debate or crisis that brings about radical examinations of conscience. There is little freedom in a Church that is in the
minority, that has been long oppressed, whose accustomed
policy is to keep silent and close ranks for the sake of unity,
to subsist and continue to live. The English bishops are rather
removed from the theologians and intellectuals in general.
Davis himself, for all of his prestige, was always kept somewhat in the background. And even though he was a *peritus*
at the Council, he was rarely consulted. His archbishop had
removed him from his teaching post in a diocesan seminary
and, according to some who were close to him, had tried to
remove him as editor of *The Clergy Review* as well. All of
this throws light on his case.

What did Davis say in his article in *The Observer?* Why
did he leave? First of all because he contested the authority
of Rome. "I found that I no longer believed in the papal
claims as defined in Vatican I and repeated in Vatican II. . . .
The Western Church was led in the course of its history to
build an elaborate institutional set-up. Unhappily the Roman
Church has made this structure an absolute. But that Church
is now internally torn by tension and incoherence, since its
institutional faith is in truth incompatible with biblical
criticism and modern theology. . . . The Church in recent
history has again and again compromised its mission to save
its institutional existence or privilege. The glaring instance
is the Church in Nazi Germany, but this does not stand
alone. When in fact has the Church ever entered into conflict with established authority to bear witness, even at the
cost of its institutional position? The Church as an institution is turned in upon itself and more concerned with its own
authority and prestige than with the Gospel message. I cannot accept its claim upon my faith."

Davis' manifesto was some sixteen typewritten pages long and was laden with such criticisms. On the primacy of authority over truth, he wrote: "Reasons of expediency, above all the preservation of authority, seem always to dominate. I look in vain at the official level for a joyful sense of the value and power of truth as truth." This lack of respect for the truth is flagrant at the Vatican: "I sometimes think there is need for a new science of Vaticanology, in order to discover which pressure groups have succeeded in getting their way and to interpret in the light of the current Roman background the more cryptic references to opinions vaguely reprobated. . . . Far from experiencing the papal authority as a living doctrinal centre, focusing, representing and sanctioning the mind of the Church, I am compelled to the admission that the Pope is enmeshed in an antiquated court system, where truth is handled politically, free discussion always suspect and doctrinal declarations won by manoeuvring." But such an attitude is not only encountered at the Vatican: "The lack of concern for truth, with the subordination of truth to authority and to the preservation of the system, pervades the whole institution. . . . The institutional Church is constantly crushing and damaging people. More and more it has become for me a vast, impersonal, unfree, inhuman system. . . . Certainly, someone should investigate the pathology of the present Church. The official Church is racked by fear, insecurity and anxiety, with a consequent intolerance and lack of love."

Charles Davis is by no means alone in thinking this way. But he followed the logic of his thought to the end: "My experience has removed the credibility for me of the official Church as a mode of Christian presence in the world. The Church of Christ is essentially the visibility of grace, namely, the visible model and witness of that interpersonal communion amongst men which is the gift of salvation. By essence the Christian Church has to be the model of human relationships and human community. When I see the official Church in its structure and activity as destructive of genuine human relationships, I can no longer accept it as the embodiment of grace. Hence I now look for the Church in the more informal groupings of Christians."

In addition to all of this, Davis announced his intention to marry. To be sure, he anticipated the objection that his tirade against the Church was no more than a desperate search for a rational justification of what was no more than the ordinary human desire to found a home. No, he said, had he simply wanted to marry he could have sought the appropriate dispensations within the Church. He asks: "What would have happened to my difficulties of faith had I not met someone with whom I knew I could share my life in deep personal love? I can only guess at what might have been, but I think that most probably I should have had a mental breakdown within a few years. I doubt whether it would have been psychologically possible for me to break out of the Roman Catholic system, in which I have been enveloped all my life and the emotional grip of which is immensely strong, without being able to turn to love and marriage for the building of a new life."

Some weeks later Charles Davis married an American, Florence Henderson, in the Anglican Church of Haslingfield near Cambridge. Today he is a professor of religious studies at the University of Alberta in Canada.

We must grant the English theologian's intellectual honesty. He admitted that his desire to marry could have influenced his decision to leave the Church. He also admitted that his marriage might render his motives suspect in the eyes of some. As a precaution, his future wife was informed of his final decision only after he had made it public. No matter. Men being what they are, Davis' witness will re-

main forever compromised (as his friend Hans Küng pointed
out) by his marriage.

The Davis case is revealing. Every time we hear—usually
indirectly through discreet channels—that a priest has decided to be laicized, someone always exclaims: *"Cherchez la
femme!"* All other reasons are automatically suspect. This is
the only one that is immediately accepted, as though priests,
and men in general, were uniquely motivated by the desire
to have sexual relations, to enter into amorous dialogue, with
a woman. It is therefore necessary to raise this question at
the outset to determine whether or not it has such primordial
importance and, if it does not, to correct the distortions it
has engendered in discussions of this problem.

The press runs stories on the marriages of priests with increasing frequency. For example, almost every European
weekly had a complete photographic report on Father Anthony Girandola of St. Petersburg, Florida. The son of Italian immigrants, Girandola is forty-one years old. He married
a woman of twenty-seven named Lorraine. He had asked the
ecclesiastical authorities for a dispensation from his vow of
celibacy. When he was refused, he married and founded an
"independent" church. Today it numbers about three hundred members, most of them divorced persons who have re-
married. The Girondolas have a son, Anthony junior. Photo-
graphs showing Mrs. Girandola helping her husband vest
for liturgical services have undeniable shock value.

Other reports from the United States announced the marriages of Father Edmund Kunth of Milwaukee to a former
nun, Shirley Weiss, and Father Frank Dewitt, thirty-three
years old, from Midland, Michigan, to Marilyn Corby, thirty-
four years old and a former religious superior. A British missionary, Father Arnold McMahon of Birmingham, married
a student nurse, Elizabeth John, without renouncing his religious state. He told the press: "God willed my marriage and

that I remain in His service. Celibacy is an invention of Rome to extend its spiritual imperialism. I am ready to fight the Vatican."

Although such reports are "sensational," they represent isolated and rather rare cases. Ordinary life doesn't make headlines.

Recently there was a controversy about a Father Weitlauf from the diocese of Versailles who, after twenty years in the ministry, obtained a dispensation from his vow of celibacy and married in the Church. His dispensation, it is true, was given on condition that he remain silent about it. Father Weitlauf did not. In our opinion he was quite justified in speaking out. Had he remained silent, all who had known him as a priest, beginning with members of his family, might have thought that he was living in concubinage outside of the Church whereas in fact his situation was perfectly regular. To accord a permission and then prohibit the recipient from talking about it publicly is an incomprehensible attitude, although this does not mean that Weitlauf should have drawn the attention of the press to his case.

We detect in such ready acquiescence to publicity a note of aggressiveness toward the Church. Weitlauf's success in obtaining a dispensation is somewhat special. But some priests publicize their marriage as though out of spite. For example, an assistant who marries a girl from the parish announces it in the local paper and settles down in the neighborhood as though deliberately trying to cause scandal. This is the attitude of an adolescent who wants to show his parents that he dares to transgress their orders to prove that he has grown up. He wants to be "recognized as an adult," psychologists tell us. And if he insists upon being recognized as an adult, the reason is often because he is not.

These sensational marriages are one thing. But priests who want to marry and remain in the ministry, and do not hesitate to say so, are something new. Petitions to the pope and bishops to rescind the law of celibacy circulate in secret. Statistics are quoted. In a survey in the December, 1966, issue of the *National Catholic Reporter*, 62 percent of the American priests declared that they would like to see an option between marriage and celibacy while 31 percent said they would marry if they were permitted to. Some months later, another survey of eighteen thousand American priests (roughly half of the diocesan clergy in the country) conducted by the American Association for Pastoral Renewal indicated that 53.2 percent of them wanted optional celibacy for the diocesan clergy. Among those in favor of this was a preponderance of young priests: 62.5 percent assistants against 38.1 percent pastors.

In India an old priest wrote that celibacy has had somewhat the same consequences as prohibition. An Italian priest told *L'Europeo* (July 6, 1967): "As a priest I must tell the faithful: come to the Catholic Church because the Catholic Church guarantees your freedom, your emancipation, your dignity. But how can I do this if the Church denies her priests the right to love another person and form a family." Father Malcolm Tudor of England announced that he was renouncing his orders to protest against the law of celibacy although he himself did not intend to marry. In Europe the Institute for Sacerdotal Assistance meeting in Lucerne in September, 1967 (bringing together some ninety experts— theologians, sociologists, university and seminary professors —from eleven nations), declared that it would be "desirable for the Church, which already envisages a married diaconate, to permit two states of life for priests as well."

Such indications taken as a whole clearly manifest the existence of a powerful movement. Another, much stronger, current of thought has in recent decades exalted the beauty and value of Christian marriage. This has undoubtedly contributed to the present explosion. Priests who preach the beauty and value of marriage to the laity not surprisingly become convinced of it themselves.

By formation and by temperament the priest is an idealist. He is especially idealistic about what he does not know: married life, for example. Intellectually he is aware of its shadows and difficulties but he does not experience them. In a pamphlet entitled, *The Challenge: A Plea for the Marriage and Celibacy of Priests,* addressed to a number of bishops during the Council, a French priest spoke unrealistically about "those laymen, in those militant homes, so committed to one another, so desirous of living their ideal in a spirit of poverty, so dedicated, so avid for the Gospel and communion, so attentive to their fellow man." Laymen have heard a lot about the grandeur of their married life and the virtues they presumably radiate. But when they consider the realities they can only conclude that their priests dream a little. Even the Orthodox Archbishop Borissov could say: "Marriage is what remains of paradise on earth" (*L'Anneau d'or,* No. 117).

As early as 1954, Pius XII, in the encyclical *Sacra virginitas,* reacted against this current. Rather than discouraging vocations by insisting on the nobility of married life, he said, it would be better to exhort married people to dedicate themselves to the lay apostolate.

This appeal does not seem to have had the desired results. Nor, judging by the reactions, does Paul VI's encyclical *Sacerdotalis caelibatus,* seem to have stemmed the present tide in favor of optional celibacy. We might even say that it has had the contrary effect. The German theologian, Hans Küng, wrote that it rather "accentuated" the difficulties and added that "there will be no peace in the Catholic Church so long as the state of celibacy is not, as it formerly was, a matter of individual choice." In the United States the Association for

Pastoral Renewal, with a membership of some 500 priests, has let it be known that it "will continue to work for the reform of the law of celibacy." In the summer of 1967 a convention of some 375 seminarians in the United States almost unanimously requested that celibacy be optional in the future. It also urged that the National Conference of American Bishops examine this problem "with renewed vigor." The episcopacy answered in November of the same year that there could be no question of this, and that hopes for a change in this discipline were without foundation. In Brazil, "official Catholic sources" quoted in the Río de Janeiro press estimated that because of the encyclical 10 percent of the 12,181 Brazilian priests left the ministry within a year. In France an opinion poll on celibacy was prohibited by the papal nuncio and the bishops. Did they fear the results? The lively reaction of the Dutch Catholics is well known. Furthermore, many priests all over the world do not believe that the encyclicals, however important they may otherwise be, are infallible.

Must we conclude that the "burden of celibacy" has become an obsession with priests? Cardinal Feltin does not think so. "The majority of priests," he says, "accept celibacy gladly, calmly and with a very real feeling of fulfillment." [1] A suitable generality for the occasion? Traces of that superficial optimism that officials like to affect? The future John XXIII wrote in 1902: "My God, I tremble when I think of how many priests violate their sacred character." At that time, it should be pointed out, his experience in the ministry was not very extensive and he could scarcely have based so general an opinion on evidence. But that was not the case in 1963 when as pope he told Etienne Gilson of his compassion for those priests who bear the burden of celibacy so generously. For some of them, he said, it was a veritable martyr-

[1] In an address to a priests' retreat, September 22, 1966.

dom, one perhaps that the Church need not impose on them. John XXIII spoke primarily of "distant continents," perhaps Latin America where it is often said that in the mountain villages "canon law no longer applies," where priests live openly with a wife and children, Here, too, generalizations are deceptive. But it is true that in Bolivia, Peru and certain parts of Mexico priests who live in isolated communities of Indians, two days walk from the nearest neighbor, do have families.

On the other hand, many priests all over the world favor celibacy. Some of them are even proud of it. But there are widespread problems as well. They are all the more serious in that little has been done—or is being done—in many countries to prepare future priests for a life in which celibacy can be fulfilling. Quite the contrary.

The feminine world? It is ignored, often deliberately. Or woman is viewed as the incarnation of Satan, the occasion of temptation, who leads man to his downfall. Because it is unknown, this world becomes both fascinating and terrifying. "Beware of women!" This cry of fear has long been effective because most seminarians, who generally come from good Christian families, have been raised with the idea that any spontaneous manifestation of emotion leads to catastrophe and is in itself a sin. They were not taught how to discipline their instincts; nor were they given any sexual education. They were merely trained to live in an atmosphere of fear.

Father Plé, a Dominican, verifies this. "In the course of examining candidates for the religious life I have been forced to recognize that, in the large majority of cases, minor seminarians, and former students of our religious houses are left in total ignorance of these questions both by their parents and their teachers. Or they are given incomplete information in a very awkward way by adults who themselves have not transcended this attitude of fear." This pessimistic diagnosis was written as late as 1965.[2]

The formation of future celibates is especially difficult in that their state of life will never be a natural one. They must be emotionally mature and be permitted to develop their own style of emotional life. They must not be de-virilized but on the contrary be allowed to have "sexed" relations with others. Curiously enough we always act as if chastity were the only virtue that must be spontaneously practiced to perfection. We admit the necessity of progression, apprenticeship, relapses and errors for humility, poverty and all the other virtues. All except chastity. Whoever is not perfectly chaste immediately, and without problems, is considered a sinner. And no pains are spared to make him aware of this.

Specialists are playing a greater role in the formation of priests today. But we are far from an ideal situation. The young priest still leaves the seminary poorly prepared to confront the world as it is for he has never known it. The feminine world that has been eliminated and ignored is forcibly presented to him in the confessional, marriage courses and study groups. The first confessions, it seems, come to him as a surprise. Relations with young women in the parish bring on his first personal difficulties. In an inquiry conducted by a group of students from the University of Louvain (Belgium), under the direction of John D. Donovan, young priests agreed that relations with young women were their second most serious problem.

In many rectories feminine presence is still restricted to a housekeeper who has reached "canonical age." But outside the rectory a priest cannot carry out his pastoral duties without coming into daily contact with women. Sometimes, as in West Germany, the housekeeper has an equal place in

[2] *la Vie spirituelle*, May, 1965.

the rectory without being morally suspect or creating a scandal. "She is without question 'the mistress of the house' and the pastor's social equal in everything not directly related to parish functions. She eats with him; they entertain together; they go out socially and even on vacations in each other's company." [3] Such an arrangement would be difficult to imagine in other countries where the priest is closely watched, even spied upon. If a woman were to occupy so prominent a place in his daily life he would be immediately suspect and very likely the occasion of scandal. But priests who live outside of the parish or their religious community are not so protected, and encounters with members of the other sex are more frequent.

A young priest coming out of the seminary, if he has any discernment at all, will soon become aware of his particular situation with respect to the feminine world. For some unbalanced and neurotic women, who usually attach themselves to their doctor or confessor, he is fair game. Others are tempted to try their luck with someone whose function sets him apart. And for some young girls who have little contact with boys of their own age he is virtually the only man in their lives.

For many women he is the only man who treats them like a human being, a person. The woman who is normally no more than an object of desire or a domestic servant soon notices that this man is interested in what she thinks, her personal aspirations, her spiritual progress. The priest is even more attractive if the woman is unhappy, mistreated or lonely. She wants to live for someone and be recognized. The priest is one of those rare men, perhaps the only one, in whom she can confide, who listens to her, who makes time for her and advises her. Perhaps she will soon feel the need for more frequent consultations and may even invent prob-

[3] Ida Gores, *Sur le célibat des prêtres* (Paris, Editions du Cerf, 1963).

lems to justify her course of action and ensure the priest's attention to her. "Many crises would not exist if the confessor were not there to hear them," said one religious. The priest is all the more likely to fall into this kind of trap because he himself is lonely.

Such was the case of Father X. He was a college professor and a good one—dynamic, popular with his students and esteemed by his colleagues. He was also a good priest, concerning himself with his students' spiritual interests, guiding them in the discovery of God, and helping them fashion an adult faith. He was, in a word, a "dedicated" man—spending his vacations with his students and thus furthering their human and Christian formation, working with them in the apostolate, preaching retreats and accompanying them on visits to foreign countries. His personal life, as far as could be determined, was without problems. He was a happy, simple and forthright man, a successful priest. Then he fell ill with tuberculosis and was hospitalized. He bore up well under this trial, so much so that he won new admiration from all who knew him. During the first year everyone came to visit him in the sanatorium. The second year there were fewer visitors, which is normal, human nature being what it is. The third year scarcely anyone visited him. When he left the sanatorium he married a nurse. He had had firsthand experience of the fact that as a priest he was alone in the world. He met a woman who was first of all a mother, soon a confidant, then a friend and finally his wife.

Exceptional circumstances are not always required for a priest to fall in love and marry. Nothing could be more normal than for a young man and a young woman, both perfectly healthy and working in the same cause, to fall in love. Sometimes they renounce the love that is offered. The young woman may withdraw out of fear. Or the young priest may be overcome with scruples or be driven into the arms of another woman. Or, again, without formally breaking the moral law, they may carry on in a state of "quasi-marriage" which is unhealthy for both the priest and the woman. There are some women who commit their whole lives to a priest in this kind of relationship. They are both companions and servants. They have none of the privileges and all of the disadvantages of a wife. They are often treated with authoritarianism; less frequently they are the dominating party. They are suspect to their friends and generally unhappy. The priest may not be aware of this at all. He simply uses the prestige that his "sacred" character, or what he judges to be such, confers upon him in the eyes of a pious woman and profits by her natural need to love and dedicate herself. When it is a question of a young woman he sometimes rationalizes. "It is better," he may say, "for her to fall in love with me. This way she won't get hurt. On the contrary, it will be easier for me to orient her toward apostolic work." Concerned with souls, he is happy to be able to dominate someone totally. These quasi-marriages are often quasi-catastrophes. Friendship with a woman is a quite different matter. In a friendship the woman is not dominated but equal. Furthermore, friendship normally leads to shared love.

When a priest and a woman love one another totally, they do not necessarily feel that they are unfaithful since God brought them together and since they very likely met in His service. In the past a priest in this situation had no other choice than live in the greatest secrecy in order to avoid ecclesiastical censure. Today priests can more easily obtain the necessary dispensations. Many take advantage of the relaxed regulations. But others postpone the moment of choice, either because they find it difficult to accept the judgment of others when they leave or because they want to remain priests. I know of an excellent priest who kept a mistress for five years and had two children by her. They lived in virtual clandestinity. It took a good deal of patience to convince him that he would be doing God's will in "regularizing" his situation.

But not everyone can, especially those who are having an affair with a married woman. But in almost all cases, human love is a trial for the priest. To be sure, a man who loves and knows he is loved generally has a feeling of fulfillment, of accomplishment, of vital exaltation. Millions of pages have been written on this theme in all the languages of the world so it is pointless to insist on it. But consider a priest who is zealous in God's service and obedient to the Church. Then he falls in love and a woman becomes the center of his life. Furthermore, he knows that he is loved. Should he renounce his love or the priesthood? After having spent so many years in preparation for and perhaps the best years of his life in the Church's service with the conviction that he was following God's will, this is no easy decision for him. A man faced with such a decision merits respect rather than condemnation, invective or scorn.

But there are always negative judgments to contend with: here is a man who chose a style of life outside the normal and ends by being just like everyone else. Those who placed him on a pedestal are angered. Those who predicted his downfall are happy to have been proven good prophets. Almost all think that he was solely motivated by the necessity of resolving his sexual problems. This is a very widespread prejudice. Thus François Mauriac wrote in *Le Figaro littéraire:* "Ecclesiastical celibacy. How can we deliver the young clergy from its inferiorty complex? One would like to be able to tell them: in no walk of life is there a more necessary victory than mastery over that madness which we must struggle against to the end of our days, no matter how long we live."

There is no doubt that sexuality has taken on undue importance in modern society. It is advertised everywhere; it enters our homes through the mass media and is currently proposed as the explanation of all human behavior. It is not surprising that priests are affected by this phenomenon. As Bishop Ancel put it: "Priests today encounter greater difficulties than formerly in remaining faithful to their vow of celibacy." [4] Even priests who favor celibacy have to exert themselves to remain chaste. Some succeed at the price of a long martyrdom. Others seek relief in masturbation, homosexuality, and so forth. Still others experience a "fall" which leaves them ashamed, discouraged, despairing. Years of laziness, dissimulated egoism and lying affect them less than a sexual slip. This is because they were taught to exaggerate its importance. They wonder whether they were presumptuous to accept the burden of celibacy in the seminary. Although not all are scrupulous. Some take mistresses and even change them on occasion. Do many do this? In his allocution of January 1, 1968, the pope spoke of the fidelity "of the great majority of the clergy." But there is really no way of knowing.

These failures are known or suspected and sometimes exaggerated. But to explain the movement against celibacy and the high incidence of priests marrying in terms of sex alone is altogether too simplistic, even somewhat insulting. This is to reduce human love to its sexual dimension. It is surprising that Catholics, who generally reject this view of love, readily adopt it with respect to the priest.

Nor can we explain all priests' marriages in terms of shared love. Father X married discreetly. He said that he wanted "to confront my bishop with a concrete situation. In the past the problem of celibacy has been all too distant and theoretical for him. Now he knows he is dealing with a real problem." Father Y also married discreetly and offered this

[4] *La Croix*, March 21, 1967.

explanation: "I am in disagreement with the Church's attitude toward the workers and her compromises with the rich and powerful. I do not accept the conditions under which we are forced to live as priests. We are overburdened with work that prevents us from going to the world of unbelievers for which Christ has given us a mandate. That is why I decided to leave the priesthood. But I also wanted to show that my decision was irrevocable. That is why I married. In the present condition marriage is a point of no return." Both priests pointed out that they did not use a woman to satisfy a principle. Rather the discovery of love for the woman they eventually married confirmed a prior decision. What was the determining factor? Only God can sound the human heart.

Father Z found himself in a similar situation. "Priests are separated from the world," he said. "They are separated by their formation, their style of life, their language, their work and even their clothing. I think that the priest ought to be a man among men and live as others do. Only on this condition will communication with others be possible. That is why I made the decision to commit myself totally to the world. And this implies giving up celibacy."

This *implies*. Celibacy is not the root of the problem. Many priests want to change their way of life because their present state is unsatisfactory. But this state is not defined only, or even principally, by celibacy. It is defined by being a priest and, moreover, a member of a social body: the clergy which has its rules, traditions, particular style of life, methods of organization and work, and customs. Contrary to the impression given by the pope,[5] most priests did not choose celibacy. They merely accepted it as a *sine qua non* condition

[5] In his allocution of January 1, 1968, Paul VI spoke of "the state which they have chosen and which is ratified by the Church" (*La Documentation catholique*, No. 1508, c. 15).

of the priesthood, a condition that is not always understood. Father Leo Trese recognizes this: "Why did we take the vow of chastity? The obvious answer is that we *had* to take the vow of chastity if we wanted to become priests, and we did want to become priests." [6] At the convention of the Institute for Sacerdotal Assistance in Lucerne, Father Vergote, of the University of Louvain, pointed out that when young men enter the seminary or a religious community, "they do not yet know what is implied in the choice of celibacy because they do not yet know the meaning of sexuality. They are not yet emotionally free." But their chances of discovering sexuality in the seminary are slim. Thus the freedom of their final choice can be questioned.

But that they freely choose to be priests is another matter. Celibacy is only a consequence of this choice, a question of Church law. As the Council said, this law "is not demanded by the very nature of the priesthood," but "celibacy has a many-faceted suitability for the priesthood." That is why "celibacy which first was recommended to priests later in the Latin Church was imposed upon all who were to be promoted to sacred orders." [7] When later, for whatever reason, they decide to leave the priesthood, they feel at liberty to abandon celibacy, which they had merely accepted or submitted to. Thus they do not leave the priesthood to marry; rather they marry because they have left the priesthood. This little recognized truth must be emphasized. The *cherchez la femme* which we hear every time a priest decides to leave is often a mistake.

Celibacy is a real and important problem. Yet it is too often discussed simplistically. It becomes a scapegoat, a fixation. "Very often," writes Father Rétif, "priests question

[6] Leo J. Trese, *A Man Approved* (New York, Sheed and Ward, 1963), p. 54.
[7] *Decree on the Ministry and Life of Priests*, No. 16.

their suitability for celibacy when what is really in question, often without their knowledge, is their suitability for other functions of clerical life." [8] We shall attempt, therefore, to analyze this predicament. And all the while we shall be asking ourselves whether it is the man who is unsuited to the role or the role that is unsuited to the man.

2

Occupational Diseases of Priests

A FORTY-YEAR-OLD man pushes a ragman's cart around the streets of Paris. His face is wrinkled and haggard. His hair is sparse and his eyes have the rheumy glaze of an alcoholic. In the winter he sleeps over the subway vents and during the summer in empty lots. He is a derelict and a former priest.

The former Father D was exempted from military service because of a slight ailment and ordained young. The son of a strict and religious army officer (his mother was dead), he followed the normal cycle from minor to major seminary. He was an exceptional seminarian—docile, full of zeal and pious. He attracted the attention of both his superiors and teachers.

At twenty-four he was named assistant in a large urban

[8] Louis Rétif, "Pour une chasteté sacerdotale plus éclairée et dynamique," *Masses ouvrières*, May, 1967.

parish. He moved in one evening in August. Two days later, on a Saturday, he took his turn in the confessional. His first penitent was a woman. Father D never forgot her perfume. It was a "magical perfume," he later told his superiors and doctors. The woman confessed sexual excesses. Father D soon realized that he was troubled and impassioned by the strange and disturbing world she revealed to him, a world he never suspected existed. Unlike most of his fellow priests, he came to like those long sessions in the obscurity of a cold Church. Listening to confessions gave him an odd pleasure. He was fascinated by evil and morbidly attracted to sin. He confided all of this to his superiors.

Various treatments and a period in a psychiatric clinic cured him, he believed, of his obsessional tendencies. But his bishop no longer wanted him. He wandered from diocese to diocese, offering his services in vain. One day he read a book about Saint Benedict Labre, an ascetic pilgrim whose neglect of his body was legendary. Father D was convinced that he was no longer worthy of being a priest. He concluded that in order to "redeem" himself he must take on the vilest human condition and abase himself totally. He became a bum.

Father D was sick. Other priests who leave are also sick. Must we conclude, as many do, that *most of them* are sick? And if this is the case, what is the cause of their sickness? These questions call for an urgent answer. For if all priests who leave are sick, their departure proves nothing.

But to answer this question we must ask two others. First, what degree of psychic health did they enjoy when they were ordained? (The answer to this question implies an investigation into the psychology of vocations.) Secondly, are not some psychological difficulties caused by the roles priests are called upon to play, thus constituting in some sense a "professional sickness"?

Thirty years ago Father Thomas Verner Moore, a Bene-
dictine psychiatrist, sounded the alarm in the pages of *The
American Ecclesiastical Review*.[1] He carefully studied the
statistics relevant to insanity and reached the following conclusions. On a representative sampling of 100,000 persons
he found 595 cases of insanity, but only 446 for the same
number of priests and 428 cases per 100,000 religious, although in cloistered life the figure rose to 1,034.

At first glance these figures seem to give a rather favorable
impression of the mental health of priests and religious. But,
Father Moore pointed out, this is because insanity resulting
from syphilis is almost totally absent in the clergy. If insanity from syphilitic cases were ignored in statistics concerning the general population, then the incidence of insanity would be higher among priests and religious than in
society at large.[2] Father Moore explained this situation in
terms of the attraction a consecrated life has for certain
pre-psychotic personalities.

Twenty years later surveys by Father Richard Vaughan,
Mother Elaine Sandra and John B. Murray reached a similar
conclusion: seminaries and religious houses attract types who
are more introverted, insecure, submissive, and retiring than
the average layman. In another study of priests, R. McAllister and A. Van der Veldt found a relatively higher incidence of social misfits than in a representative sampling of
laymen. This phenomenon is not peculiar to the United
States. About the same time in France, Father H. Gratton,
an oblate of Mary Immaculate, observed that "too many
candidates for orders and those already ordained suffer from
psychological troubles." [3] The attraction of a life in religion

---

[1] "Insanity in Priests and Religious," *The American Ecclesiastical Review*,
Vol. 2 (1936), 484–498.
[2] Similarly for alcoholism. Father Moore found 20.74 percent of alcoholics
among priests against 7.3 percent for the male population in general.
[3] Supplement to *la Vie spirituelle*, No. 42 (1957).

for those whose psychic health is deficient is no longer seriously contested today.

Many authors have spoken of "sheltered vocations" to describe those who remain infantile or adolescent in their behavior, who are afraid of the world, the great adventure of life, or professional and family responsibilities. They see the priesthood as a way of avoiding such responsibilities as well as the difficult struggle to acquire professional competence. In the seminary they are not obliged to take a degree. There they are protected from everything that might threaten their pusillanimity.

Some of them feel a profound sense of inferiority. They are in search of compensations, of something that will enable them to give meaning to their lives. Membership in the clerical body—solid, organized, hierarchical—provides security, and the respect that members of the clergy still enjoy gives them a feeling of personal worth.

Others need to shine, to be singular. They are attracted by the rituals, in which the priest plays the lead role in the Christian assembly, and by the liturgical vestments. Concerning these a seminary superior said, "They think they have a vocation to the priesthood when in reality they are more qualified to be sacristans or the bishop's valet."

The list is long. There are anxious types in desperate search for an assurance of salvation. Others are burdened with a sense of psychological guilt and seek at all costs to expiate, "to make reparation." Still others are afraid of their sexuality. "Sexual silence, which is to say the absence of apparent sexual desires and problems in a young man of twenty, is not normal and certainly no cause for rejoicing. Such silence, to say the least, is no guarantee of positive virtue. It is in fact a neurotic repression. It is understandable why such a young man is invincibly attracted to religious life in which the problem of sexual behavior is *a priori* settled. Not only is he asked not to have sexual contacts but is further requested to fight against any eventual desire. Thus he is crowned in his own eyes with the prestige of 'holy virtue.' Such motives, believe me, are more frequent than one might suspect." [4]

The schizoid, withdrawn into himself, the passive personality and the paranoid who overestimates himself and despises others are also attracted to the priesthood, the first type because he will be "set apart," solitary, the second because he desires a way of life in which nothing but obedience is asked of him, the third because he can speak in the name of God and be invested with a quasi-magical power to denounce the world. These unconscious impulses do not exclude conscious motives that are praiseworthy and supernatural. But their importance is beginning to concern the responsible authorities, superiors of seminaries and novitiates who are intent upon detecting false vocations. The Apostolic constitution *Sedes Sapientiae* (1950) defined a vocation theologically as a double call: the divine call which constitutes it and the call of the Church which ratifies it. The second call, according to traditional doctrine, is based on two essential qualities in the aspirant: the right intention and the necessary talents. No one has the right to be a priest. Only the Church has the right to choose those whom she calls to the priesthood and lay down the conditions.

In former times she was not very demanding. Arguing that many workers were necessary for the harvest, she accepted—and still does in some seminaries and religious orders—almost anyone who presented himself as a candidate. In 1936, however, Pius XI wrote in the encyclical *Ad Catholici Sacerdotii* that "one well-formed priest is worth more than many trained badly or scarcely at all. For such would

[4] Romain Matignon, *Vie consacrée et équilibre psychique* (Toulouse, Editions Edouard Privat).

not be merely unreliable but a likely source of sorrow to the Church." Today concern is being shown for the unconscious motives of a vocation, and since 1950, Roman documents have proclaimed the necessity of good psychic health and sufficient maturity in candidates for the priesthood.

In France a document published on June 23, 1966, under the auspices of the Episcopal Commission on the Clergy and Major Seminaries enumerated the following signs of "human immaturity" and warned seminary superiors to be on the alert for them:

—Excessive submission and dependence, or nonconformism and instability;
—Withdrawal into self and the inability to put oneself in the place of another;
—Intolerance in one's judgments and rejection of reality;
—An incapacity to accept adult responsibiilty and carry something through;
—Excessive emotional involvements;
—In the domain of sexuality, fear of the feminine world, contempt for sex, or, what is more frequent today, idealization of woman and marriage.

"Any one of these symptoms," said the document, "could indicate immaturity. It should serve as a warning, and the convergence of several symptoms is cause for alarm."

In the United States all dioceses and religious orders (and in Europe a good number of them) now call upon specialists to determine the psychological aptitude of candidates. These psychological examinations, which include interviews and tests, can take different forms. Sometimes they are conducted by a psychiatrist or by a priest psychologist. More frequently they are supervised by a team which includes a priest, who may or may not be trained in psychology, a psychiatrist, who is also a doctor or a psychoanalyst, and a psychologist. These specialists do not determine who shall be admitted to the ministry. They have no power of decision and merely point out to the candidate himself or his superior (as is more often the case) his psychological characteristics and possible danger signs. Two organizations have been created in France—the AMAR (the Medico-psychological Association to Assist Religious) and the AMAC (the Medico-Psychological Association to Assist the Clergy)—to administer these examinations, help priests in difficulty, train psychologists and organize further research.

But this is a recent trend. The large majority of priests have never been subjected to psychological examinations.

Many priests suffered from their psychological problems while they were still in the seminary. Studies conducted in the United States on priests under psychiatric treatment show that they were aware of serious emotional problems, sexual difficulties, problems in their relationship to their superiors, pathological scruples and crises of anxiety before they were ordained. In some cases their superiors counseled them in vain to give up their ambition to become priests. In others, they were not aware of the gravity of the problem or even encouraged the seminarian to persevere although he entertained doubts about his vocation.

Father M was the last child of a large family. His mother and father were "good Catholics" and active in several parish and diocesan organizations. At fifteen he was a brilliant and pious student. His family, his teachers and his pastor encouraged him to enter the priesthood. In the major seminary he suffered a nervous breakdown. But he carried on with his studies and was eventually ordained, although he spent half of his time in the seminary on sick leave. After ordination, failing to get the position he desired, he suffered another nervous breakdown. He rebelled against his bishop and his mother, accusing both of them of neglecting him. He wrote to his mother: "You spend so many hours visiting the sick of the parish yet you have only written two letters to your tired son." For years he was unable to say Mass. Doctors said he suffered from a typical persecution complex. Father M's difficulties were evident while he was still in the seminary. But his superiors chose to close their eyes.

It is generally much easier today to leave the seminary, although not always. There is a recent case of a young man who was reluctant to enter the seminary because he was not sure of his vocation. But he was advised to give it a try. He finally accepted. In the major seminary, just before he took the habit, he experienced further doubts. He was persuaded that this step was not a decisive one and that his seminary life would be more honest, loyal and complete if he wore the soutane like everyone else. Thereafter, despite his protests, he was always treated as a future priest and assured that his difficulties would pass. He was discouraged from taking a leave of absence to reflect on his problems. Step by step, the young man (whose personality was obviously not very strong) was convinced that he was called to the priesthood. He was ordained in due course.

Would that such sad adventures were no longer possible today. But they are.

In 1960 the Roman Congregation on Seminaries addressed a stern warning to the bishops of the world: "We must regrettably acknowledge that despite strict instructions from the Sacred Congregation on the Sacraments—*Quam Ingens* (December 2, 1930) and *Magna Equidem* (December 27, 1955)—many are still admitted to sacred orders who do not have a true vocation. Nor is it a question of humanly unavoidable errors. In reviewing the history of many failures it has become obvious that clear indications of the lack of an ecclesiastical vocation could have been discerned while the subject was still in the seminary." [5]

[5] Letter on the occasion of the third centenary of St. Vincent De Paul (September 27, 1960).

A fairly large number of priests, who desire despite everything to remain faithful to their commitment, think that they should have left the seminary. "Courage in the seminary would have been to leave," says one thirty-eight-year-old priest. "The atmosphere in the seminary was such that there was no turning back; since I did not know life I wasn't free," reports another. As far as can be determined, neither of the priests here quoted had any special psychological problems.

In a situation where everything was designed to prevent candidates from leaving, we can easily understand why superiors were little concerned with dismissing those who were neurotic or prepsychotic, even when they were aware of their personal difficulties. The expressed desire of the candidates to become priests was considered a sufficient motive to keep them. If they were unlucky enough to be brilliant, even further efforts were made to prevent them from leaving. Of course "further efforts" must be qualified by saying that this has not universally been the case. Analyzing priests under psychiatric care in the United States, R. McAllister and A. Van der Veldt observed that 48 percent of those hospitalized had been highly gifted students and 16 percent were above average in intelligence. As a result of their study they recommended to seminary authorities not to look only "for intellectual qualities in candidates because emotional maturity is not necessarily related to a keen intelligence."

But we must be careful not to lay all the blame on seminary superiors. They were also victims of the system, subjected to the absolute control of Rome, and liable to reproach from the authorities and their colleagues if their institution registered an unusually high number of departures.

McAllister and Van der Veldt also found, in agreement

with most serious studies on this subject, that seminary life in the past exacerbated psychological troubles. They affirmed, and the paradox is only apparent, that candidates who were psychologically healthy experienced neurotic guilt feelings because of their inability to lead the abnormal life of seminaries perfectly while candidates who were psychologically abnormal were highly esteemed by their superiors because of their successful adaptation to this abnormal way of life.

The responsibilities of seminaries in the Church are great. The Church ordains men who are in principle adults but in most cases were children when they were initially recruited. The charge of rearing them to adulthood was thus transferred from their parents to the seminary. But in the past the authorities were more concerned with turning out men who were obedient, punctual, zealous and faithful to the exercises of piety, than with strengthening their personalities. Because seminarians were forced to live an artificial life, their maturation was retarded even though they might have been perfectly normal to begin with. The result of the seminary influence has been succinctly summarized in the harsh judgment of Joseph Folliet: "They are still wet behind the ears," he said of the seminarians he knew in concentration camps.[6]

In 1965 the American priest, Robert Brooks, wrote: "When seminary authorities define candidates as immature and in need of constant surveillance, when their disciplinary policies are obviously predicated upon a deep distrust of human nature and a negative concept of chastity, and when they allow little room for initiative and decision-making they are creating a stifling institutional climate in which normal per-

[6] Quoted by R. Matignon, *op. cit.*

sonality growth becomes exceedingly problematic." [7] One
year earlier a seminarian in eastern France answered an
inquiry in these words: "It is time that we stopped treating
men in their twenties like kids. I remind you that a seminarian is a person. But in the seminary there are no responsibilities; no initiative is possible. What is stressed is sacro-
sanct obedience, the fidelity of a dog." There is a curious
unanimity of opinion on both sides of the Atlantic.

Today seminaries are in the process of realizing their
aggiornamento; they are less closed and authoritarian. The
rather dark picture we have just sketched explains the difficulties of many contemporary priests. But in many countries
it no longer corresponds to the reality. Since the Council,
many happy changes have taken place. The Congregation
of Seminaries, which in the past has exercized a meddle-
some and retrogressive influence, has had to give in to the
many criticisms directed against its policies. The Synod has
given new life to these reforms. No one, of course, wants to
see authoritarianism replaced by laxity, and there is no doubt
that the pendulum often swings from one extreme to the
other. But that is another story.

The seminary system of the past (and in some cases, of
the present) is therefore largely to blame for the high incidence of psychological problems among the clergy. But
often these problems do not manifest themselves until after
ordination. This is not surprising. The clergy are no exception
to a rule very familiar to psychiatrists: the signs of neurosis
become evident with the first responsibilities of social life.
Suddenly the young priest discovers the real problems of
men from a source other than books, the "cases" of his

[7] Robert Brooks, "The Sociological Dimensions of the Seminary," in James
Michael Lee and Louis J. Putz (eds.), *Seminary Education in a Time of
Change* (Notre Dame, Fides, 1965).

manual on morals, or theoretical discussions. Suddenly he
sees that his own problems are unresolved. Disturbed himself, he is called upon to help others. This will prove to be
too much for him if he is still "immature," if part of his
psyche is still at the infantile or adolescent level. Then his
neurosis will become apparent.

Not all "immature" young priests become neurotics. The
crisis they experience in the beginning of their ministry helps
many of them grow up. But it is still regrettable that their
maturing process is so slow. Regrettable and dangerous, both
for them and for others.

Moreover, the state of life they have chosen does not
always help them attain psychic maturity. An adult is one
who accepts himself as he is, with his limits. This is a difficult frame of mind for a priest whose ideals are high, who
desires to be a "bridge" between God and men. He envisages
this role with passionate enthusiasm only to risk a feeling of
impotence and discouragement when he comes into contact
with everyday reality.

The adult is one who is capable of determining his role
in society, usually through the profession he exercises. The
priest could do this in former societies in which his social
role was clearly determined. But today it is increasingly
difficult to do so.

The usual responsibilities of an adult are those of family
and profession. The lack of these responsibilities retards the
maturity of the young priest.

To be sure, he has other responsibilities. Indeed, without
any particular training he can suddenly find himself charged
with building projects, teaching, the administration of youth
centers, and so forth. There is a case of a young assistant
who was assigned to administer two large summer camps
and found at the end of the vacation that he was in debt by
several hundred dollars. Rather than tell his pastor he foolishly

decided to rob a butcher shop. The butcher surprised him in the act and, as an enlightened Catholic, took him to a psychiatrist rather than the police. This is a somewhat extreme case. But, burdened with responsibilities they are unprepared for, young priests often withdraw into themselves and seek refuge in prayer because they are afraid of contact with men or—as often happens in educational work—devote themselves to children because they are afraid of adults.

The true adult is liberated from aggressive reactions which are the reflexes of childhood. But the priest's immaturity makes him hostile toward his superiors and others. Such priests evince an intransigent dogmatism, judge mercilessly, are enthusiastic about new pastoral and liturgical experiments, making each one of them an absolute and untouchable value—until the next one comes along. Many Catholics today rightly reproach them for this hard passion and intransigence. Unfortunately, they are often the same Catholics who defend the traditional seminary system, as though it were equally absolute and untouchable, without understanding that it was this system which made their priests aggressive and infantile in the first place.

Most priests succeed in overcoming these crises. Others are caught in a terrifying dilemma. They see their beautiful image of the priest crumble into a thousand pieces. Feeling total failure, they experience great difficulty even in carrying out the tasks of their "trade"—hearing confessions, distributing communion, and so forth. They doubt their vocation. "I am not capable of being a good priest," they think. "I am a bad priest, I am betraying those who counted on me, I am causing them harm. Perhaps I should never have become a priest in the first place. I made a mistake, I didn't have a vocation. I may not even have the faith." If they continue in the role of priest, they feel like hypocrites. This makes them all the more aggressive. Anyone who feels guilty, whether rightly or wrongly, tries to transfer the responsibility for this guilt to others in order to escape his obsessive feelings and inner chaos. Then they perversely accuse their parents or their educators, their bishops or their pastors, of having misguided and misunderstood them. Sometimes, of course, they are right.

At the same time it becomes increasingly difficult for them to bear up under the frustrations of their way of life: the frustrations of celibacy—which is not only the renunciation of carnal pleasures but also emotional loneliness—and the absence of intimacy and tenderness which union with God in prayer does not always compensate for; frustrations related to poverty and obedience; frustrations originating with the world's respect, or lack of it, for the priest.

At this point the priest frequently finds himself in the psychiatrist's office. The intervention of psychiatrists coincides so frequently with priests' departures that they have been sometimes accused of advising or at least encouraging them to leave. But psychotherapy can do nothing to remove a genuine feeling of guilt. It can only liberate the subject from neurotic guilt. It makes him face himself, look at himself honestly when he would prefer to criticize the institution, the priesthood, the Church in order to avoid making an honest judgment about himself.

In any case, the evidence furnished by psychiatrists on the genesis of psychological troubles experienced by priests is extremely valuable and revealing. Here is a summary of their reports: [8]

1. Almost all of these priests received a strict, moralistic education. The Christian religion was presented to them as a

[8] The interested reader will find further developments in a report published by the authorities of the former psychiatric clinic at Cambo (Lower Pyrenees) which was opened especially for priests. The report, signed by Dr. Parrot, Father Romain Matignon, Miss Mabille and Father Courtelare, was published in Vol. 46 of the Supplement of *la Vie spirituelle*, 1958.

law and not the grace of faith. They were taught that sin was an infraction of this law rather than a lack of love. "In catechism classes," said one of them, "they were always talking about sin. When I was nine years old my pastor refused to give me absolution because I watched the dancing at a local festivity through my bedroom window."

2. Their sexual education was nonexistent. Sex was a taboo subject in their families. Yet it was the principal subject matter of confession. The priests asked so many questions about it that the penitent more often than not failed to understand what he was suspected of.

3. A large number of these priests were subjected to the influence of a rigid and scrupulous mother. It was often she who urged them to become priests, who chose for them.

There is the case of a young boy who contracted meningitis when he was three. His mother made a vow that he would become a priest if he were cured. Later, she reminded him of her vow so often that he came to believe no other course was open to him.

Here is another case. A seminarian stole a chalice. The seminary authorities were very puzzled by this surprising gesture on the part of one whose record was unblemished and who, moreover, did everything possible to get caught in the act. It turned out he simply wanted to prove to his mother that he could not be a priest. He knew that she wanted this more than anything else in the world. So he fabricated a way of proving to her that he was unworthy.

Pious women imagine that by offering a priest to God they consummate a sacrifice divine love demands of them. The close emotional ties between a mother and her son often serve to orient the child toward the seminary. Women who are unhappy in marriage try, often unconsciously, to spare their sons the experience of conjugal life. Widowed mothers with an only son can be sure that as a priest he will never "belong to anyone else." Women who at one time aspired to the religious life project their unfulfilled wishes on their children. Widows who have been left alone by the death of their husbands find their son's ordination an occasion to shine socially.

In the beginning of the century and until recently the Church encouraged these attitudes and constantly appealed to the mother's influence. Nor were the noblest sentiments always evoked. Consider the following text: "The life for which a mother prepares her son is the highest and noblest because it is closest to God. It is also the happiest. . . . She will not have to worry about his food or clothing since Christ has promised to provide for his disciples. She also guarantees herself an honorable and comfortable old age, for to give her son to the priesthood is not to lose him but rather to keep him. *He will never give his heart to another, a mother may be assured, God will be the only one he loves more than her.* A mother acquires eminent rights in heaven, for to offer a priest is much more meritorious than to give a glass of water to one of the Apostles." [9] True, this text dates from 1912. But for decades articles, pamphlets, lectures, pastoral letters, sermons, novels and even popular poems harped on the same theme.

As late as 1947, Canon Chauvin published a book entitled *A Mother's Dream* which appealed in the same way to maternal egoism: "Your little one will come back to you. . . . You will always be his mother. . . . You who desire support will always have your child near you. He is yours alone." In 1955, J. Van Agt wrote in *The Mothers of Priests:* "He will remain in his mind and heart close to his loved ones, and since his heart is pure he will love God alone more than his parents." In 1956 a vocation display in Paris offered prizes for

[9] Report by Father Legrange to the Diocesan Congress of Bourges, published in the *Revue de Clergé Français* (Paris, 1912).

the best posters. Six of them portrayed the priest's mother
(offering her child, praying, etc). Only one depicted the
father and mother reading the Gospel together, and none
of them showed the father alone.[10]

Perseverance in this line of propaganda bore fruit: Many
vocations were recruited from among mothers. Their sons
later inherited them. Some of them became good, happy
priests. But not all. Most of them would never admit that
their choice had been forced on them. For example, a fifty-
two-year-old priest with serious problems shouted to his
psychiatrist: "I have been told that my mother forced me
into the priesthood. That is not true. She always told me: if
you are going to be a bad priest, don't stay in the seminary."
Then, overcome with emotion he added, "You see, I have
been a bad priest," not realizing that he contradicted his
previous statement by admitting that he was still afraid of
disobeying his mother, that she still dominated him.

Today the Church is less deferential to mothers. But the
maternal influence on vocations remains strong (which does
not mean that it always is bad). In a survey conducted in
the diocese of Malines-Brussels (Belgium) priests were
asked what the most determining influence on their vocations had been. Thirty-five percent answered "a priest" and
30 percent said it was their mother.[11] In the United States,
John D. Donovan studied the background of Catholic college
students and discovered that a representative number of
future priests recruited from among them described their
homes as authoritarian and characterized by strong emotional ties between mother and son.[12]

The death of the father or a divorce in the family can also

[10] Quoted by J. Rogé in *Le Simple Prêtre* (Paris, Casterman).
[11] Ricardo Seidel, *Actitud del Clero Diocesano de Malines Bruselas ante el
cambia social* (Catholic University of Louvain, 1966).
[12] John D. Donovan, *The Academic Man in the Catholic College* (New
York, Sheed and Ward, 1964).

a3se

S

predispose a young man to the priesthood. In such cases the psychological process of growth is disturbed. After weaning, as is well known, the child normally goes through an Oedipal stage which is characterized by a strong emotional attraction to the parent of the opposite sex. To attain psychological maturity the boy must go through a second phase of identification with his father.

His admiration for his father will determine how he later plays his role as a man in society. Without a father he will encounter great difficulties in this role unless he finds some other man to take his father's place as an object of admiration. Until he has gone through this phase he will remain to some extent infantile. The priesthood can then become a refuge for him, an excuse to retain a close emotional relationship with his mother that no one will disturb, a means of avoiding competition in professional life and manly encounter with others.

These are not mere suppositions. A survey of major seminarians in France in 1967 indicated that 40 percent of them came from abnormal homes. In 22 percent of the cases the father was dead; in 4 percent of the cases both parents were dead; in 12 percent of the cases they were separated; in only 2 percent of the cases was the mother dead. The father's absence thus seems to favor vocations to the priesthood.

Some qualifications are not in order to give a more balanced picture. We do not mean to imply that priests who come from normal homes are exempt from psychological troubles or that vocations from abnormal homes ought to be *a priori* suspect. The latter are by no means all "immature," nor are all mothers of priests guilty of violating their sons' freedom. What is true is that the abusive and decisive influence of some mothers and the lack of father identification can sometimes adversely influence vocations, cause psychological troubles and eventual defection. A superior of a major seminary who had a good deal of experience went so far as to say that "most" of the priests he had seen leave were from disturbed families.

4. The testimony of psychiatrists also reveals that the majority of patients were labelled "future priests" from their childhood. Their development was uniquely oriented to this end, so much so that normal human fulfillment was frustrated. Even when on vacation from the seminary they were "set apart" and forbidden to participate in the normal activities of young people of their age. This situation has much improved in recent times. But most priests in the ministry today were formed before seminary reform began and consequently could not benefit by its liberating effects.

5. They received a clerical formation that was too idealistic. They were presented with a magnificant portrait of what a priest should be—a kind of superman, omniscient, capable of speaking with authority on all subjects, able to lead men in all situations, without faults or weaknesses. But when they found themselves in the real world among real men, they were forced to admit that they bore little resemblance to this ideal. Then the more scrupulous of them asked: Did I make a mistake? Am I a sinner? Have I lost the faith? They had fallen from the pedestal on which they had been placed.

6. Most of them do not know how to pray, or pray little. In any case prayer is not a joy for them, a moment of relaxation or comfort in intimacy with God, but a duty they perform mechanically, without love. "One has the impression that for many of them neurosis would not have manifested itself had they known how to pray." [13]

This list is not complete. We have not mentioned, for example, psychological difficulties which are caused by the priest's relation to ecclesiastical authority, or his style of life,

[13] Cambo report, *op. cit.*

or loneliness. We shall examine these questions separately
and in more detail. But these omissions in themselves show
how difficult it is to separate the genesis of psychological
difficulties from everything that makes up the life and role
of a priest. The following chapters will endeavor to demonstrate this.

For the moment, let us attempt some tentative conclusions.

The claim that most priests who leave are psychologically
sick is absolutely unverifiable in the present state of research.
It isn't likely that we will ever have completely reliable statistics in this domain. That a good number of those who leave
have consulted a psychiatrist is true. This doesn't mean that
they are sick. But they are upset, and often there is no one
with whom they can discuss their problem frankly. To leave
is always a difficult thing to do and they seek assistance.
Some of them even try to avoid responsibility at a time when
they are calling the whole course of their lives into question.
They would be greatly relieved if psychiatrists would tell
them that they are not responsible for what is happening to
them, that the psychological circumstances of their childhood and formation years are to be blamed.

Even if most of them were sick, we could not conclude—as
some would like to do—that more discrimination in the beginning would suffice to avoid what the Congregation of
Seminaries calls "shipwrecks." Nor can we conclude that the
departure of sick priests proves nothing. On the contrary,
three conclusions seem to be indicated:

1. The ministerial priesthood, as it is lived today, has a
definite attraction for the immature, the prepsychotic and
social misfits. Happily, its attraction is not limited to these.
But what are we to think of a way of life that exercises this
kind of appeal?

2. The seminary system, as it has been organized until

now, causes or aggrevates psychological problems for many candidates to the priesthood.

3. The priest's way of life today, far from alleviating these problems, sometimes transforms them into serious crises or provokes new ones.

What are we to think of this situation?

The following chapters will try to answer this question and furnish more evidence for our third conclusion.

3

The Problem of Loneliness

IT WOULD BE desirable to have reliable information on the order of importance of the reasons why priests leave: the desire to marry, false vocation, loss of faith, financial problems, difficulties with authority, etc. But it isn't likely that we ever will. Total honesty in this domain is rare. One priest leaves to marry and advances theological justifications; another who has serious psychological difficulties explains that he is exercising his natural right to found a family. Machines could easily enough tabulate the explanations offered but they cannot judge their sincerity or truth.

In the absence of such information we can nonetheless affirm with some certainty that loneliness is a major factor in most departures. This is typified by the material loneliness of many country pastors. The Church is so organized that priests have to stay in the country when everyone else is moving to the cities.

Father M was one such priest. He didn't want to go to the country even though, as was pointed out to him, it was a promotion. He explained that he was born in the suburbs, the child of a working class family, and knew nothing about rural problems. He wanted to stay in the city, even at the price of remaining an assistant for the rest of his life. At the time he was thirty-four years old and happy as a member of a team of five priests in a large urban parish. The bishop explained that he needed more dynamic young priests in the rural parishes. "And anyway," he said, "you won't be there more than a few years. After that we will find a nice parish in the city for you." The assignment to the country was, as it were, a trial period.

Faithful and obedient, Father M accepted. He left his youth organizations, a pastor whom he loved very much, and Gerard, another assistant, who was his closest friend. He courageously took up his new duties. And, so it seemed, with considerable ability. His lanky frame soon became familiar to the country folk. He organized the young. He was seen in the cafés of the village and often lent a hand to the farmers in the field. He was on good terms with the agricultural unions in the area. Each summer he rented a bus and took his parishioners on pilgrimage. In the spring he accompanied young people to other parts of the country to improve their education. He seemed perfectly adapted and relaxed. The chancery officials congratulated themselves on an excellent choice. Who could have guessed that Father M found the loneliness of his life, especially the trial of Sunday evenings, unbearable? One of these Sunday evenings determined his future. It was six o'clock. Father M put the car in the garage and closed the doors. It had been, like all Sundays, a long day. "After all, it's the only day you work," a parishioner had once said to him, half humorously, half seriously. He said four Masses in the morning, had two baptisms in the afternoon and a meeting with a girls' club after that.

Father M went into the empty gray rectory. There were eight large rooms, not counting an immense attic. Since he lived alone, he only used two of them: his bedroom and a combination dining room–office. He lit the stove and turned on the radio, as he did every evening. Night was already falling. It was winter and the house grew cold and damp as rain beat against the windows. The priest picked up a newspaper. His cat, which had been asleep on the armchair, stretched and began to rub against his legs. This animal, a gift from one of the local farmers, was the only living creature Father M would see all evening. His parishioners were at home, after a day of visiting with relatives. He had seen them silhouetted against the curtains on his way home. They were watching television, playing cards, enjoying themselves together. But he was alone with the silence of the evening. Sunday was the worst, especially in winter. During the week he had meetings or dined with a family in the parish. But on Sunday he thought it more prudent to absent himself. In the summertime he could walk in the woods or work in the garden until it was time to go to bed. But the rigors of winter forced him inside early. He turned the radio up to fill the silence and it carried echoes of a life he felt excluded from. Silence had finally become intolerable.

Three years earlier Father M couldn't have suspected the existence of the Sunday night trial. In the city Sunday evening had been a moment of relaxation. Dinner was a joyful time as the five priests talked over the busy day. They had worked hard and were now content, like laborers after a heavy day's work. Later he and Gerard would go to the movies or visit with friends to smoke and talk. They returned to the rectory exhausted but alive.

Here a cat was his only companion. His nearest colleague, a priest of some sixty-odd years, had resolved the problem of the evening by going to bed at seven o'clock. Another, also up in years, had become a television addict. When he first came to the parish, Father M had hoped to collaborate with the neighboring pastors. They could have worked together, perhaps even lived together, serving their parishes out of a central headquarters. But they refused. "At our age we are set in our ways. Impossible. We are old bachelors, a little on the fussy side. We cherish our independence." And so it went. Perhaps they liked their loneliness. In any event Father M realized it would be useless to insist.

Loneliness had become a familiar terror to him. He was not afraid of the day. He could always find something to do. He liked manual labor. He also liked to meet people, listen and talk to them. But in the evenings everyone went home early. And Father M would dread the rebirth of loneliness. Especially on Sunday.

On the advice of his confessor—his former pastor—he tried a number of devices to combat his fear. Intellectual work, for example. For weeks he had studied theological manuals. But as soon as he lifted his eyes for a moment he would realize that he was alone in the empty, silent house. He could have cried had there been anyone to hear him. He also tried prayer. He spent hours on his *prie-Dieu* fingering his rosary and meditating. But he remained "dry," as they say, "it" wouldn't come. It was difficult to pray. It was as though the external silence caused interior tumult. "My God is this what you expect of me? Why this ordeal? Is this really your will?" A flood of questions. Certitudes crumbled into doubts.

This Sunday evening Father M broke down in tears. For a long time he had resisted. But tonight he cracked. Why tonight? Did he know himself? He had simply had enough. Father M spent a disturbed night. He went to the Church and prayed for a long time before the altar. Then he wrote some letters. One of them was to Gerard: "I can't take it any longer. You will be surprised. And perhaps feel let down. But try to understand. I am convinced that the Lord doesn't demand this of me. I don't have a hermit's vocation. I simply wanted to be a priest. But the silence is overwhelming. The silence has broken me. It is more than I can bear."

When Gerard received his friend's letter he went to the chancery office immediately. He demanded that they do something for Father M—get him help if he was suffering a depression, another assignment, anything. He was told that Father M had asked to return to the city six months earlier and was refused. Three months later he asked for permission to go as a missionary to Africa or Latin America. But the bishop had personally ordered him to stay in his own diocese. Anyway, they told Gerard, it was too late to do anything now. Father M had left that Monday morning without a forwarding address.

To conquer his loneliness—but didn't his loneliness really conquer him?—Father M chose an extreme solution. He left everything. Today he is married and works as an accountant in Paris.

Loneliness, which sometimes leads to alcoholism, is by no means limited to country pastors. Cardinal Feltin of Paris has said: "In an urban diocese like our own, distance is no problem. Yet many of our priests suffer from both physical and moral loneliness: the young who are not warmly enough welcomed and encouraged and the old who are tempted to discouragement or worn down by criticism." [1]

[1] In a speech to the priests of Paris, September 25, 1965.

As Cardinal Feltin suggests, there are several kinds of lone-liness: physical, emotional, moral. But all forms are equally dangerous. And all of them give rise to the same disturb-ances, except in those rare instances in which loneliness is turned to spiritual gain. The evil is well known. Perhaps this is why many young men prefer to enter a religious order.

It is not good for man to be alone. In order to find fulfill-ment he needs the group. Man must feel loved and esteemed. He must also love. To love one's work is not enough. Emo-tional exchange at a personal level is also necessary. The priest is no exception to this universal law.

Some argue that the love of God is enough. They are ad-mirable theoreticians. For how can the love of God be sepa-rated from the love of men? They talk as thought it were possible to renounce human affection without suffering emotionally, as though it were possible to love God when our hearts have dried up. The strictest orders in the Church establish communities.

Today, of course, many secular priests live together in one form of the apostolate or another. This is all to the good. But it is still too limited. Moreover, it is no cure for a funda-mental aspect of the priest's loneliness: the widespread feel-ing that he is on the margin of the world and life. In ana-lyzing this problem we are raising the whole question of the priest's place in our society.

The feeling that life is passing them by is expressed in every inquiry or interview conducted among priests. One complaint, which is perhaps too extreme, nonetheless sums up many others: "Because I have been forced to flee reality, reality flees me. I am on the margin of things: thou shalt not know a woman, thou shalt not work with your hands, thou shalt not engage in temporal pursuits, thou shalt not be like the rest of the world, thou shalt be always apart. Not to be able to live is hell."

Sometimes even seminarians have this feeling of isolation. One superior of a major seminary put it this way: "Many seminarians who enter young feel they have been 'plucked' too early. They are haunted by a nostalgia for a human life which they will never know and are sometimes inclined to idealize the world. What are the implications of this? What effect will the cloistered life of the seminary have on a young man today?" [2]

For those who adapt easily to the artificial life of the seminary, the suffering of loneliness will explode later on with greater force. It will then take on a different coloration, for the priest is no longer sheltered. He lives in the world. But he is out of place there.

It has not always been so. In pretechnological society the priest was perfectly integrated.[3] In the stable world of former times, tradition was an important social factor and the role of the priest—*presbyteros*—was precisely to transmit this tradition. Society then was hierarchical and divided into "estates." No one questioned this hierarchy. The chief values were obedience, resignation and submission. The clergy was one of the higher ranking "estates." Its authority was not contested. Men of lower estates would not dream of rebelling against authority. The clergy felt no need of justifying their superior rank. It was in the nature of things. The poor world, where technology had not yet wrought its marvels and was in fact undreamed of, was of little interest in itself. It was a "valley of tears." Unable to master things, man attributed mastery to God, a God who was understood as an almost direct cause of all natural phenomena. The priest was the mediator between this God and the world. He was a kind of "heavenly sorcerer," in the magical sense of that word, and

[2] Albert Uguen, Superior of the Major Seminary at Quimper, in *Christus*, July, 1967.
[3] On this subject, see in particular Jerome Régnier, "Principales difficultés des prêtres dans un monde en mutation," *Vocation*, No. 236.

was accordingly an important person in society. He intervened in daily life because he possessed powers which other men did not have.

The Church was at ease in this world. She developed as a clerical society rather than as a people of God. This world gave the priest social status, a distinct profession, privileges (such as exemption from military service), and a livelihood from the Church. To be a priest was to have a precisely defined and recognized social function.

Democratic and technological society put an end to this. It fostered a sense of human autonomy and the value of terrestrial things. It introduced the idea that truth requires research. Man cannot simply obey a system imposed from without. It analyzed natural phenomena and proved that they obey scientific laws, have a certain autonomy and for that reason do not depend on God's constant intervention. The world is not a place of pilgrimage but a home we build to live in. In technological society the sacred is merely a part of existence, it no longer pervades life as such. Consequently, the man of the sacred is not quite a whole man.

Saint-Simon's "parable" might clarify the priest's difficult situation in modern society. In 1819, Saint-Simon said that modern technological society needed new leaders. The former leaders—lords and clerics—no longer served any purpose. "The loss of 30,000 of the supposed most important leaders of the state—members of the royal family, cardinals and archbishops, clerics and magistrates would perhaps cause sentimental regret but would not seriously endanger the state," he wrote. On the other hand, "suppose that France suddenly lost 50 leading chemists, 50 leading bankers, 200 leading businessmen and 600 leading farmers. The nation would become a body without a soul and immediately fall into a state of inferiority." It is understandable why Claude-Henri Saint-Simon was imprisoned. He announced the reversal of the order of values and denied a useful social role to the manor lords and pastors. The manor lords were soon forced to capitulate. But the pastors resisted. The whole nineteenth century and the first half of the twenieth century until the Council (in some cases a little earlier than this, depending on the country) were characterized by the clerical society's desperate effort to survive. The Church withdrew into herself, inviting those who kept the faith to enter the ghetto. "Outside the Church, no salvation." The Church, in this expression, was usually understood as a clerical society, emphasizing the separation between the clergy and the world and trying desperately to retain control over the Church which it had appropriated in the pretechnical era.

But it wore itself out in this effort. Until the beginning of this century membership in the clergy still guaranteed a recognizable social position. Today that is no longer the case. Those who still believe it does, and their numbers are rapidly diminishing, and attach themselves to outmoded titles and fancy clothing do not realize that they are in most instances pathetic figures.

In Germany the bishops of the Rhineland ordered an investigation into the reasons for the vocation shortage. The survey reached this unanimous conclusion: "Neither clothing, ordination, studies nor celibacy can guarantee the priest an assured and esteemed position in society." In the United States, where religious roles traditionally have had great social prestige, a similar phenomenon has been noted. Opinion polls on the relative prestige of the professions show that between 1947 and 1963 the Catholic priesthood dropped from eighteenth to twenty-first place (out of ninety professions) and Protestant ministers dropped from thirteenth to seventeenth place. This is all the more remarkable, the American authors point out, in that this pattern "is contrary to the general tendency of the liberal professions." All the more surprising too, we might add, in that the Church in America does not have a feudal past.

Another striking example is furnished by the former Belgian Congo. During the long years of colonial rule only the religious institutions enabled the natives to achieve positions of responsibility and prestige through the priesthood and episcopacy. But independence opened up an immense field of new possibilities—in the civil service, politics and even business. A considerable percentage of seminarians then opted for other professions. The social status of the priest has not perhaps diminished but it has lost its exclusive character.

Within the Church the importance of the clerical society and the prestige of the priest have also diminished. As Michael Novak—one of the founders of the National Association of Laymen which came into being in June of 1967—put it: "The Church, to paraphrase Clemenceau, is much too precious to be left to the clergy." This remark is revealing, even though one must guard against attaching too much importance to it.

Formerly, the lay state was looked upon as a concession to human weakness. In the twelfth century Pope Honorius II wrote that "the Church has always offered two ways of life to her children: one to sustain the weakness of the infirm, the other to perfect the happiness of the strong." Today, of course, the lay state has greater prestige. In modern society one rarely excels in more than one field because it is now impossible to be polyvalent. The priest has become exclusively the man of "religion"; his interference in other fields is not accepted.

Many priests feel left out. They can no longer participate in social, economic or political activities without being accused of stepping out of line, even though they are citizens. Camilo Torres, a Colombian priest, at thirty-six asked to be laicized in order to engage in revolutionary activity against poverty, the United States and the landowners. His case raises a number of questions—especially the question of a theology of violence—and clearly exposes the following contradiction: in order to remain faithful to what he believed to be the profoundest demand of Christianity, Father Torres was obliged to renounce his ministry because it made him a "religious" specialist.

Side by side with the tendency toward specialization there is a tendency toward less specialization (everyone, for example, drives a car), toward a higher educational level that is available to increasing numbers. Consequently, the role of the specialist in religion is diminishing. Almost any educated layman knows more theology than the average pastor. We are tending toward an individualization of our faith. As the world becomes more socialized, the idea that each individual must discover the meaning of his own life and the answers to the problem of his destiny is gaining ground. Each time the institution of the Church is contested as the guardian of the deposit of the faith, charged with announcing the good news to all nations and handing down a tradition from generation to generation, the status of the priest, as a functionary of the Church and a specialist in religion is, at the same time, attacked.

This evolution is in many ways very positive. Few, for example, take exception to the Council's reaffirmation of the place of the laity in the Church. But it was inevitable that this rediscovery, following upon centuries of the Church-as-a-clerical-society, necessitate a more precise definition of the priesthood, that it embarrass the priest, even though he dare not admit it.

Many laymen in the Church today are fighting against clericalism, and some priests are encouraging them. Both resist the theory which holds the priest to be the absolute sovereign of the community. The laity want their voice to be heard and they are not always tactful in expressing this desire. Priests are only too glad to listen to them because they have become aware—with an awareness that is sometimes excessive—of their ignorance in other fields. But even in the most progressive parishes clericalism is by no means dead. The liturgy is changed without consulting the "consumers." The first liturgical reforms after the Council should not have been carried out without consulting the parishioners. But the list of those parishes in which this was done would be a short one, unless of course we were to include those pastors who only consult laymen who agree with them—by no means a rare phenomenon.

Clericalism is hard to kill. Its longevity, it seems, can be explained by the following three reasons:

First of all, the priest is permanent while the layman, however much he may participate in the life of the Christian community, remains a benevolent amateur who has other preoccupations and responsibilities. The priest who is charged with the day-to-day life of the community is easily tempted to take whatever decisions he deems necessary for the community by himself and to look upon prior consultation with the laity as a needless delay. Secondly, despite recent progress, the priest still considers himself, often with good reason, as a "specialist." In principle the layman is not. The priest who gets new pastoral ideas in journals and study sessions might well fear that any initiative would be rejected *a priori* by poorly informed and incompetent laymen if they were consulted. Consequently he prefers to assert his own point of view.

The third reason takes us to the heart of the matter. Clericalism is widely denounced but never replaced. So much so that the priest is in some sense mutilated. His authoritarianism and incursion into fields where he has no competence might be viewed as compensations for the frustrations which the sacerdotal condition as it is lived today impose upon him. One might, for example, write at length about clerical authoritarianism toward nuns, which seems to be a direct consequence of celibacy. To prevent the priest from being clerical without changing anything in his way of life is to make the latter even more unbearable. That is why so many priests, with the best intentions in the world, unconsciously give into the clerical temptation. A desire for absolute control, an attitude of assumed importance and a scarcely concealed vanity—these are the cleric's besetting sins. One must live as best one can.

Another recent development in the Church has strengthened the priest's feeling of uselessness. The Church at Vatican II not only admitted the influence of the world but also gave evidence that she is capable of renewal and fresh ideas. Timidly at first, she "recognized" the new world with its autonomy and consistency. This aggravated the priest's problem since he had always defined himself in relationship to what was not of the world. The layman did not have to reconvert when the Church recognized the world; he had already participated in its creation. The victim of the Church's new understanding of her relation to the world (and we have only seen the first stages of this) was indeed the priest.

He is a victim of a double movement and contradictory demands. On the one hand, his former role as a "model" has been rescinded and he is looked upon as nothing more than a ritual minister. He is less and less able to function as a social being, devoted to the community, or as an amateur psychotherapist, because specialists have taken over these roles. Except in matters theological, and in some rural communities, he can no longer pretend to be a man of knowledge. He is thus obliged to redefine his position. His flesh, as it were, has been eaten away, reducing him to a skeleton. But this flesh had held him together. Now he must seek a new purpose. Indeed, he must ask himself: what is a priest today? There is an abundance of literature on this subject.

On the other hand—and this is the second trend—the priest, even though he no longer enjoys a special social status or can claim special knowledge, remains the man who affronts the limits of knowledge, who measures himself against the obscure forces of death, who deals with realities that cannot be put in words. He must prove his mastery of these realities by personal virtue. Men today are gradually casting aside traditional morality. But the more they liberate themselves, the more they transfer moral demands to the person of the priest. He has become the guardian of the morality of their ancestors and not the minister of the Son of God who was made man and lives forever. The Christian communities share this way of looking at things. An inquiry conducted among Catholic Action workers in Belgium showed that they expected the priest to practice above all the natural virtues: honesty, frankness, respectability, courage and so forth.[4] They want their priests to be endowed with all the virtues. This is because the group recognizes itself in its chief. If the leader is perfect, the group feels "valorized," as the psychologists point out. They have more self-esteem when they know they are led and loved by such a man. But if he shows any weakness, the group feels that its honor is compromised and its stability threatened. Thus the chief has no right to be weak. He cannot be mediocre.

The attitude of the hierarchical Church reinforces this bias. It readily and perhaps unconsciously puts the priest on a pedestal. It does everything possible to cover up his faults. Acting thus, it strengthens the priest's feeling of being apart, different.

---

[4] J. Rémy, "Les milieux proches du clergé et l'image qu'ils ont du prêtre," in *Sacerdoce, clergé et changement social* (Louvain, Center of Socio-Religious Research).

The man-priest is imprisoned in a network of prohibitions by the self-appointed defenders of the letter of the law. This is a difficult burden to bear. He always feels that he is being watched and judged, considered both as an oracle who always speaks the truth and at the same time as one who understands nothing, who represents an outmoded mentality that does not speak to modern man.

"Men want you," wrote Karl Rahner, "when you come in the name of God and are yet a man. They want more brilliant messengers, more convincing heralds, more zealous hearts. They readily accept men who are assured of success, who have an answer and a remedy for everything. Terrible illusion! Those who come are weak men who walk in fear and trembling." [5]

If priests are conservatives, they resent the criticism of those who would deprive them of their former role as leaders in society and confine them to the sacristy. If they are progressives and reject the traditional image of the priest as a dealer in magic whose religiosity does not result in an authentic Christian life, they are more sensitive to the criticisms of those who would restrict them to their traditional role.

In either case the priest feels he is more a personality than a living person in the eyes of others. And his personality sets him apart.

But every man needs to be "recognized" by others. Recognition, psychologists tell us, is necessary to the fulfillment of the young. For adults it is a necessary condition for participation in social life. The priest suffers from not being recognized as a man. His desire to be human is not merely to satisfy a natural and legitimate desire—for as a man he belongs to the human community. As a priest he must become part of that community in order to preach the Gospel. Thus the isolation imposed upon him is doubly intolerable.

[5] Karl Rahner, *Sur le sacerdoce* (Paris, Editions de L'Epi).

The former Father R who left the clergy and yet felt "more a priest than ever" declared: "At last I can communicate with people who see in me the person and not the personality. They confide in me without fear and without complexes and I can speak freely to them. My present experience is basically like that of priests who were prisoners during the Second World War and have indelible memories of the time when they were truly men among other men."

4

They No Longer Know Who They Are

"THE CRISIS of the priesthood? I can sum it up in one sentence. It is a question of those who no longer know what their profession is, for no one has taught them. No one can teach them because no one knows what it is. Yet priests are told that this profession will fulfill their lives."

The priest who spoke these words is an influential figure. His smile testifies to his robust optimism. But this does not prevent him from seeing clearly and speaking frankly.

"When I was in the seminary," he continued, "we were taught how to administer the sacraments and teach catechism. At that time—almost fifty years ago—they had begun to speak of 'winning souls.' But nobody worried much about this. The young priests of my generation thought they knew what they had to do. They were also convinced that it made sense, not only for them but for their future parishioners as well. But many of them were mistaken. They were reduced to celebrating marriages and funerals and teaching catechism to youngsters who were completely indifferent to it, as though they were actors in an unconvincing morality play. And they were told that these activities should fill the emptiness of their celibate hearts and occupy all of their time. What is admirable is that so many of them have persevered —silently.

"Priests today no longer know what their role is. They are taught theology in the seminary but it is a theology that is uncommunicable to the people because it is more cerebral than ever. They are also taught how to administer the sacraments. But the 'consumers' don't want them, or they want them in such a way that priests are obliged to question the seriousness of these rites. The merchandise, if I may speak familiarly, priests have to sell is continually being called into question by exegetes and intellectuals.

"No longer knowing what to do, they try to save face by bold innovations and specializations. They do not understand that the priesthood as such must be discovered anew. Or they blame the bishop. After all, he should know something. But he doesn't. When he talks to his priests he usually avoids the real questions because he doesn't know what the answers are."

There is nothing particularly new here. Twenty years ago Canon Boulard quoted to a congress the disturbed letter of a country pastor: "It would be desirable to conduct a survey among priests, asking: 'What is your mission?' 'What contribution do you have to make?' We can imagine the varied answers. Is it possible that we priests don't have a very clear idea of what we are supposed to be doing? Our first loneliness is an inner hesitation, doubt, uncertainty, the fear of what others think." [1]

This pastor didn't go so far as to admit that he didn't know what to do. Twenty years later priests are forced to acknowledge the obvious. In all fields of their endeavor, even the least contested, they feel that they are woefully inadequate.

Everyone recognizes their role as cultic ministers. They acquit themselves of this role with commendable zeal, often very concerned with "liturgical renewal," and desirous that the expression of faith be more authentic, more living and more communitarian. But they cannot help observing that their efforts do not fill the Churches.

The sacraments are frustrating. A father asks to have his child baptized or a young couple wants to get married "in the Church." But the priest has never seen this father and only vaguely remembers the engaged couple from catechism classes. He questions them and soon realizes that they merely want to go through a formality that has no real meaning for them. What is a sacrament that is no longer a sign? If the priest refuses to give the people what they want, he risks being misunderstood or breaking the thin thread of contact with his flock. Often enough they can get what they want in a neighboring parish that is less demanding. Yet if he gives in, he feels that he is betraying the seriousness of his function.

Sermons are a trial. He would like to communicate all of his faith, uneasiness and hope to his congregation. But the congregation's attitude infuriates him. As soon as he begins to speak, their attention wanders. Their sad, polite faces cannot hide their total indifference to what he has to say.

Catechism classes are a cause of despair. He has tried all the new methods. But he notices that when children have finished the obligatory classes to which he dedicated his time

[1] A report in *Evangelization* (Paris, Editions Fleurus).

and efforts, they forget everything connected with the catechism. If at least he could only be sure that he had implanted in them a desire to go deeper or an aspiration. . . .

The lay militants console him. He sometimes is inclined to admire them the more in that he has few other sources of satisfaction. But he asks himself: What exactly is a Catholic Action chaplain? How does he help young people define their faith through action? How does he distinguish his role of firing the faith of front line soldiers from that of those who work with the rear guard? He feels that he is in some sense betraying them by constantly urging them to a kind of action he can never participate in himself.

In former times he had other consolations—his educational, charitable, cultural and athletic activities. In cultivating these he felt he was acquiring a speciality, creating something, almost exercising a profession like everybody else. But an increasing number of priests reject such a role today. It isn't our work, they explain. Such activities keep Christians in the ghetto. It cuts them and us off from others—those we no longer see in parish organizations or at Mass, those who do not send their children to parochial schools.

The "others" whom he does not reach, with whom he is unable to establish a dialogue—the nonpracticing Catholics, atheists—are a source of profound anguish for the priest. He feels he has been ordained for them. But he despairs of reaching them, with a despair that is all the more profound in that it is not only the consequence of a professional failure but of an emotional frustration as well. Because he is isolated, the priest attaches supreme importance to contacts, to personal relations.

Some, it is true, seem to rejoice in their misery. They constantly harp on the new needs of the modern world and its rapid evolution. They continually predict a rising tide of atheism. Even their successes seem doubtful. They are always disposed to criticize as sentimental folklore what may be expressions of a sincere faith on the part of simple people. In their eyes, every practicing Christian is *a priori* suspected of insincere motives, unless of course he shares their malaise. They are fond of comparing the statistics of different parishes, as though the worst record were the most enviable. They seek desperately to formulate means of dialogue with men and make every effort to adapt their language, but end by forgetting what they want to say. Dialogue—a word that is so overworked that it has no precise meaning—is their ideal, but how can one dialogue effectively if he has lost faith in the truth which dialogue serves? And how can one hope that dialogue will be an effective missionary instrument if one is not happy being what one is? Dissatisfied, such priests announce crises, which the Church hopes to surmount purified and finally rejuvenated, as final catastrophes.

Often harsh in their judgments of others—except atheists or those who have broken with the Church—they fail to conceal a strange lack of confidence in themselves. They are no longer too sure of who they are, and that is why they no longer know what to do.

Priests who rivet their attention on their uncertainties, who are petrified with anxiety, often tempt the laity to say, and not without reason: "Come now, my dear Father, a little common sense. Don't dramatize matters. Things are not so simple or so uniformly black." The priests might answer that it is easier to compromise when one has not committed his whole life. What they probably won't say, although it is true, is that their attitude can also be explained by their formation. The priests were taught to be scrupulous rather than optimistic, to cherish the absolute over the relative, to be more concerned for perfection than happiness. And happiness in this world (which priests should have a right to like anybody else) is compatible with a serene acceptance of one's failures.

Most priests, moreover, do their best to transform their failures into successes. They read the journals and attend conventions in an effort to find solutions to their problems. They are concerned with experimenting. They try to acquit themselves of routine duties, which they believe in less and less, because most Catholics and their superiors expect this of them, and at the same time work for the evangelization of unbelievers, which they consider their primary mission. But it is a wearying role. "We are always chasing after a solution we can never find," said one pastor. "What is tiring is not so much what we do. It is rather what we would like to do and cannot. We go to conventions and leave with so many questions that we cannot sleep at night. To keep asking oneself what must be done cannot be tolerated for a whole lifetime."

Priests expect new directives from the authorities. But when they come they are appended to the old ones. They don't replace them. Everything becomes a matter of priority. Each priest then chooses among the priorities—alone or in collaboration with others who think as he does.

Not all priests have the same inclinations. A given pastor will readily speak of "options in the parish" although they are as a matter of fact more his than those of his assistants. The clergy gives the impression of a disunited organization in which one group criticizes another. Dissension is more common in difficulties than in success. A survey among country pastors indicates that a third of the clergy are satisfied with the "traditional" apostolic methods; another third want "modern" methods; still another group favor "experimental" methods; and, of course, there are those who think that the situation is hopeless, that no method will be effective.[2] This is not new, of course. But that fact doesn't make it any the less serious. In 1955, Pius XII made this pessimistic observation: "When we note the fervor of so many initiatives

[2] Jacques Maître, *Les Prêtres ruraux* (Paris, Editions du Centurion).

in which everyone gives unsparingly on the one hand and on the other the paucity of results obtained in relation to what one would normally expect from so great an expenditure of energy and such sacrifices, one wonders whether we are not working too much alone, isolated and disunited."

Not only do priests not know what they should be doing but they give the impression that they do not know how to organize what they are doing. Disorder reigns at all levels. A parish priest finds it difficult to follow a schedule. With few exceptions he does not know in the morning what he will be doing in the afternoon. His day is made up of "bits and pieces" which he tries to put into some kind of order: meetings, administering the sacraments, administrative work, catechism classes, counselling, evening meetings. It takes a good deal of will power, given such dispersion, to resist the temptation to laziness. The absence of an organized work program, moreover, scarcely favors good health. Many have had to seek treatment for this very reason.

Some progress, of course, has been realized in this matter, especially where team work among priests leads to a certain division of labor, the beginnings of organization. But many priests, under the fallacious pretext of being all things to all men, do not divide their time equitably among prayer, work, study and meditation. Usually study and meditation suffer. Sometimes prayer as well. It seems as though they fill their day with routine tasks thus to avoid getting a perspective on things and asking some difficult questions.

The nature of the priest's work makes it difficult to organize. But it is not impossible. A better use of the clergy as a whole would be an improvement. For the disorder we speak of is not merely an individual phenomenon. In Paris a short time ago two priests in the same parish died of overwork. But many priests are virtually unemployed in the same city.

In a diocese in northern France the ratio of priests per Catholic population varies from one to ten, i.e., from 352 persons per priest to 3,623. On a world scale the statistics are even more depressing. A diocese in Brazil has 14 priests for 400,000 baptized Catholic whereas the diocese of Coutances in France has 600 priests for about the same number. "No government in the world utilizes its personnel as badly as the Church," Bishop Kaiser of Peru said at the Council. But it wouldn't do to send some of the clergy from Coutances to Brazil. These priests would be limited in what they could do since they are alien to the Brazilian mentality and problems. Nonetheless such a disproportion is shocking.

This question has been debated for years, but the results are negligible even at the national or diocesan levels. The uneven distribution of clerical manpower is one of the principal reasons why priests get discouraged. "If an engineer considered our situation, he would think we were all crazy," wrote one young priest. And he continued: "I have only been ordained seven years but I have already suffered much. I pray that the Lord will be merciful to others who suffer as I do. The priests of my generation? They are overworked and badly employed. They feel useless. But they have little time to think about their problems. I have seen many of them take 'sick leaves.' For nothing, absolutely nothing, has changed. We no longer know what to do or how we should organize or how to live."

This professional disarray is further aggravated by two difficulties that priests rarely mention in public: the system of promotions and their financial difficulties.

What? Do priests concern themselves with advancement like civil servants or corporation executives? Pious souls may be indignant. But priests do indeed concern themselves with this. Not that most of them entered the clergy with careerist intentions. If this is what they truly wanted, they would no doubt have chosen another walk of life. But advancement—promotion to pastor, for example—gives them more status in the eyes of others as well as their own, that necessary feeling of their own worth, more autonomy, more meaningful responsibilities (think, for example of those who are still assistants at the age of fifty), and guarantees a certain material independence. Promotions, however, are determined by unspecified and unsatisfactory rules. In the United States, Arthur X. Deegan studied what factors are important in naming pastors and found that in 61 percent of the cases it was "seniority," in 14 percent of the cases "administrative experience" and in only 7 percent of the cases "personality." Many pastors told him that it was "an indefensible and intolerable system, a tragic error that does the Church much harm." In France there is a trend away from promoting priests on the basis of seniority, although this rule has the merit of clarity. Today many priests think that it is of primary importance to be known. Thus the role of public relations becomes correspondingly significant. "A minimum of good public relations is an important factor in promotions," we read in a bishop's report to his priests. Ability is not enough. The priest must also make his ability known.

The priest who fails to get the responsibilities he hoped for may try to hide his disappointment. But this deception soon leads to others. Disappointment is all the more difficult to bear because it is considered, wrongly, as something shameful. A false conception of humility prevents many from talking about it openly.

The financial problem is equally secretive. One report notes that "there are three kinds of questions that are never discussed sincerely and openly among priests: their spiritual life, emotional difficulties and financial resources." Nor are they discussed with laymen—except to ask them for money without showing them the books. Shame is one reason for this reticence. It is not easy to admit one's poverty. It is still more difficult to admit that one sometimes lives by humiliating and embarrassing means—donations from one's family or relatives, pilfering collections intended for other purposes, gifts, tips, produce (in the country) and so forth.

The fact is that the basic salary in most countries where priests are financially responsible for a Christian community without state aid is paltry and inadequate.[3] This forces them to adopt expedients that create shocking inequalities among the clergy and contribute to the persistence of a serious problem.

The outcome of this, at least, is clear. Priests do not even benefit from the esteem their voluntary poverty deserves. One Frenchman out of two couldn't say how priests live. There is much criticism of the clergy's supposed love of money, but material difficulties are not even suspected. One pastor of a small parish lives with his mother (who draws a small pension) and a crippled sister (who has some health insurance). He makes so little that he is obliged to cultivate a large garden in order to live. When his parishioners see him at work, they say: "Aha! Getting a little exercise, hey?"

The modern world advertises the basic elements of comfort in an obsessive manner. The priest is not immune to this publicity. He, too, desires comfort. Yet he is criticized for enjoying comforts that others take for granted

Not all priests can tolerate so difficult a predicament. Some leave uniquely for this reason, although they rarely admit it. They can easily find more convincing justifications. It is by no means honorable to leave the priesthood because of money. Not honorable, but nonetheless understandable. In

[3] The situation is obviously different in the United States where many priests live in bourgeois comfort. But this raises other problems.

France, 60 percent of the Catholic population contributes less than twenty francs per year to the support of their clergy.[4] Let them cast the first stone.

For those who remain, poverty, or the humiliating means they take to overcome it, makes the professional crisis more critical. When a profession pays an adequate wage, its members are better able to cope with the difficulties they encounter within it. If their profession were more rationally organized, priests would not feel so inefficient. If the possibilities of their career were more clearly defined, they would be less impatient. If their efforts were equitably distributed, they would be encouraged. Because this is not the case—or rarely is—priests find their apostolic failures increasingly difficult to bear. They cannot satisfy their need (one that is common to all men) for effectiveness and success, especially those who have a technical mentality. Two kinds of crises result. One is traditional and well known. It afflicts priests in their middle years. The other, more recent, is more likely to afflict priests who are conservative and inimical to change.

At forty, the priest's future in the Church is pretty well determined. With few exceptions, he knows then what promotions he can still expect and what positions he can aspire to. It is difficult to get "a second wind." As a young priest, dynamic and enthusiastic, he gave of himself unstintingly. He lived a veritable honeymoon with his parish or school. An older priest has remarked humorously that there are "graces of blindness for youth." Then the day comes when he must admit that his efforts did not achieve the results he had hoped for. He catches himself thinking that his active life is already nearly over. At forty or forty-five years of age one wants to be sure of his bearings. But this is not always possible. "The balance sheet of my priestly life is a balance sheet of failure. May the Lord forgive me for being a bad

[4] Enquête Sofres, 1967.

priest." The future is a cause of fear. "A whole lifetime always beginning the same things over and over again, with a hope that is always shattered by the facts, forever facing the same failures." Priests almost never find in the exercise of their ministry a satisfaction commensurate to the sacrifices they have made.

The most generous and zealous of them experience serious crises (although some are spared by reason of their deep spiritual lives or commitment to the apostolate). At such moments all of their emotional problems surface at once. Loneliness is most keenly felt. Many then discover their sexuality and the feminine world for the first time. An exacerbated sensitivity clouds their vision of reality. They are inclined to dream, to dramatize, to idealize. Will they rediscover celibacy at forty as some men rediscover their wives at the same age? Not necessarily. Some will leave to marry. The "noonday devil"—another scapegoat—is generally mentioned by way of explaining such cases, thus ignoring the fact that it is a feeling of priestly failure, the uncertainty of what to do, that makes them leave.

Although it sometimes comes to the same thing, the crisis of "the conservatives" is quite different. Attached to methods which they are now told are old-fashioned, they are reluctant to accept others whose efficacy is by no means evident to them. And changes in the Church seem to them to involve much more than methods. They had accepted *en bloc*, a package deal as it were, a system of dogmas, rituals, customs and theological presuppositions. If certain customs and presuppositions are questioned, they fear that the entire edifice will fall into ruins. "In face of all these changes which they sometimes think are too numerous and too sudden," Cardinal Leger, then archbishop of Montreal, said in 1966, "some priests may be tempted to panic and discouragement. Many of their certitudes seem to have collapsed. They had lived in a more immobile world. On the moving ground where they now find themselves they no longer feel secure as they once did."

Some adopt the "integralist" attitude which holds that to change anything is to invite total catastrophe. They observe that obedience does not pay. The innovators, those who took official directives with a grain of salt, have finally after twenty years been vindicated. After having disavowed them, the authorities now ratify their experiments. It is always like this, they reason, when reformers are given a free hand and the central power does not keep a tight rein on its men. To open the door an inch, in liturgical reform for example, is to invite the bold to go one step further. They are in the avant garde, not in error. Those who obey, on the other hand, have the feeling of being behind, outmoded.

The conservatives are not always older priests. A survey in Belgium indicated that age is not a determining element in a priest's attitude toward the Church.[5] The formation he received is of much greater importance. Those who were for years subjected to the "dos" and "don'ts" of the seminary are lost in the bracing air of *aggiornamento*. "In a number of workshops with priests," writes the American psychiatrist E. Mark Stern, "I have met many who do not accept change as a basic part of their lives." [6]

Some leave. "I was told to embrace all sorts of values and activities to give meaning to my life. Now they are rejected. Thus I no longer have any reason to sacrifice my life."

It is not surprising that this crisis of the conservatives is most frequent in those countries where Catholicism, often a minority religion, was for centuries fixed in a strict mold: Canada, England, the Flemish countries, Latin America, etc.

---

[5] R. Seidel, "Orientations au changement du clergé de Malines-Bruxelles," in *Sacerdose, clergé et changement social, op. cit.*
[6] *Jubilee,* February, 1967, p. 191.

But the "professional crisis" of the priest is universal. And it is often expressed in accents of hopeless resignation. Some try to explain it in terms of a loss of faith among priests. This is a somewhat simplistic diagnosis. It is precisely because they have faith that they seek desperately for a more effective way to communicate it. If their faith were not strong, many would leave who continue to work silently, trying to forget their uncertainties, who bear up under their anxiety and cultivate in spite of everything a small flower of hope.

5

The Bishop in the Defendant's Box

A SINGLE SHAFT of light filtered through the partly opened shutters and illumined the dark room. When he first entered, Father G hesitated to sit down. He walked about, looking at the pictures on the walls. The bishop's predecessors in their red and purple robes looked down stonily from their ornate frames. These grim reminders of death intimidated Father G. So did the silence. Outside there was a large garden and a high stone fence separating the bishop's palace from the street. It was a dead street, lined with old houses that seemed to be all inhabited by elderly people. It was the oldest section of the city. It had once been the center, but the axis of activity had long since shifted. Father G had some difficulty finding the place. He was more familiar with the chancery

office in the downtown area. As he sat uneasily on the edge
of an armchair, it occurred to him that in his fifteen years as
a priest this was his first visit to the bishop's residence.

He had met the bishop on the occasion of annual retreats
or confirmation tours—a good way this is, his first pastor
had explained, to force the bishop to visit his parishes regularly and keep in touch. They were, to be sure, quick encounters. After the ceremony the bishop chatted for a half
hour with the priests in attendance and then excused himself: "I still have five hundred children to confirm today. A
demanding schedule, but I was most delighted to see you.
Come to see me another time."

Father G had first heard this invitation two years earlier,
just before the Council opened. He heard it again when the
bishop presided over a meeting of some twenty priests who
had gathered to discuss problems of the apostolate. The
bishop had again extended the invitation: "Come to see me
another time."

Why should anyone want to go see him? Father G wondered. After all, who knew the bishop? He had come to the
diocese six years ago from the other end of the country. Just
why he had been named to this particular see remained a
mystery. Chance perhaps. It was rumored that four or five
others had been offered the post but turned it down because
they thought it too difficult. A bishop is supposed to be the
father of his priests. But Father G and many of his colleagues
found it hard to take seriously a paternity that was based on
the subtle machinations of episcopal promotion. The new
bishop was a cautious man, one accustomed to making his
timidity look like prudence. The priests could not be convinced that their diocese had been confided to a man of
sterling qualities. But Father G had enough faith to accept
him. After all, a bishop chosen from the diocese might not be
any better. The first few years were difficult, but eventually

the new bishop succeeded in dissipating some of the reservations among his clergy. On the whole he conducted the affairs of the diocese with relative efficiency.

One reason why priests rarely visit their bishop is the fear of attracting attention to themselves. What would his colleagues say? Father G knew very well what they would say: that he was "pushing himself," that he was looking for a promotion or trying to land a cushy job, one of those diocesan positions—children's groups, women's organizations, the press, or whatever—that gave one a speciality and removed him from the drudgery of parish work. Father G had remained deaf to the bishop's invitation for more than two years. Then one day he made up his mind. He had conducted funeral services in the morning. After he had prayed over the casket and expressed his condolences to the family, the idea suddenly came to him: go see the bishop and tell him how it is. Father G knew that the bishop received visitors every Tuesday from three until seven. Today, as it happened, was Tuesday.

After lunch Father G drove the thirty-odd miles to the diocesan seat. He wanted to be early because there would likely be others waiting. But no. A surprising calm reigned. In fact there was no evidence that anyone else would be visiting the bishop that day. A young priest-secretary answered the door and ushered him into the waiting chamber. "Please wait," he said before disappearing.

Father G felt like a prisoner. Had he dared he would have opened the shutters. Perhaps the sunlight would have dispelled the gloomy fascination of the portraits on the wall. He had the impression he was being judged by a long line of apostolic successors.

As he waited, he rehearsed the little speech he had prepared. "Your Excellency, things aren't going too well. I was fifteen years old when I decided to become a priest. I have never since doubted my vocation. I knew what I wanted to do: announce God to men. I was impressed by an article in one of the youth magazines that spoke of France as a mission country and said that thousands of our countrymen have never heard of God. I asked: why not me? This desire has always sustained me, although the seminary years were rough.

"After my ordination I was named as an assistant here in the city, at St. X's. You know it well although you never met my pastor, Monsignor B. A fine man. He took an interest in the good health and comfort of his assistants. He loved me, I am sure. But he was quick to throw cold water on my enthusiasm. "Young man, he said, put the parish before unbelievers. Our parishioners have first claim on your services." Putting the parish first meant, for example, spending three months of the year organizing the annual festival. The Monsignor was a master of ingeniousness when it came to something like this. He was also a man of stout virtue. He feared no sacrifice. In his old age he would go on sick calls in the middle of the night and take the early Mass each morning. But we didn't see eye to eye. I waited. I told myself that when I became a pastor I could do things my way. Meanwhile, patience. It befitted an assistant.

"I have been a pastor for seven years now. But it isn't working out. I have failed to be the kind of priest I wanted to be. My parish—or rather my parishes since, as you know, I have three of them—are devouring me. The liturgy, funerals, marriages, catechism classes—I try to do everything as best I can. But it takes all of my time. I have some youth organizations, one group of women and a few men that I meet with from time to time. I try to get them into Catholic Action. But you have no doubt observed how difficult it is to get people in these parts to do anything. I tell them that they are responsible for evangelization, that they must

announce God to unbelievers and be bearers of the Word.
And me? I stay where I am with this fire burning in me because I have no time. Or more exactly, in what spare time I
do have I meet with unbelievers. A few of them at any rate.
But I know full well that I do not succeed in entering into
real dialogue with them. I lack the proper vocabulary. For
them I am a pastor and so they construe everything I say as
a sermon. I cannot dialogue as one man to another. Consequently they don't really listen to me. They only pretend to
out of politeness. I have reflected on this matter at length
and I know that there are others who have the same problem. And so I have come to ask a favor of you. I have never
done this before. I do not want to be a pastor because I want
to be a real priest. Find me a position in a factory, in Africa,
Latin America. It doesn't matter. I will do anything to be a
real priest. I won't even ask for a choice. Send me where you
will."

Father G was rather satisfied with his little speech. He had
even prepared answers to objections he anticipated. For example: "Don't tell me that pastors feel they aren't real
priests?" Answer: "Some do. I am not trying to lay down a
general rule. I am presenting my personal case. I find it impossible to be both a pastor and a priest. I have been a pastor
for seven years and this has been my thinking for six of them.
I have suffered this problem for a long time and tried to do
my work as a pastor honestly. Now . . ."

A door opened. The bishop entered. He was dressed in
black. After the Council he had given up purple, except for
his skull cap. This is a good man, thought Father G. The
bishop's face was attentive and smiling. But it was also dis-
tracting. "This man may be good," Father G said to himself,
"but I do not know him. How do you tell someone you don't
know who is also your employer what you have never confided to anyone? And how will he judge me? Like a father?

It is said that a bishop is a father to his priests but I knew my father well. I lived with him for many years and yet there were times when I found it difficult to confide in him."

They sat down facing each other in the large office that opened out on a sun-drenched garden. The bishop went on smiling:

"I am very happy to see you, my dear Father. It is a great joy for me to meet with my priests. We should do it more often. This is my most ardent desire and it is yours too. I know it is. I have a good deal of respect for you. I know you are doing good work. One of your parishioners, a lawyer, told me this just a few days ago. He doesn't appreciate all of your innovations [the bishop's smile grew more pronounced, more benevolent, at this point], but he recognizes your ability and dedication."

Why go on? This was a lecture and not a dialogue. The bishop continued: "I am told of your negotiations to have the Church repaired. Drive a hard bargain." He expressed concern for parish life: "Keep up the good work in catechism classes. This is the essential. I am told your methods are interesting. If you are criticized, say that I support you." And, finally, a few platitudes on the lack of faith: "So many young people don't practice. This is a terrible burden for me. The diocese has lost the faith. But we must not give up hope. Emphasize Catholic Action as much as possible. We must have confidence in the laity. There are some admirable militants among them." At this point Father G, somewhat stunned, recalled snatches of his speech. He wanted to say: "This is precisely what I came to talk to you about, Your Excellency."

"My dear Father, our work is not always rewarding. But it is essential."

Father G left after a half hour without explaining the purpose of his visit. The bishop hadn't asked him, thinking perhaps that he had come on a social visit, which called for casual conversation.

Three months later Father G wrote to inform the bishop that he was leaving the priesthood. "I am going to work in a factory where I can be a real priest. I can't be one within the present parish structures."

Does this story sound unbelievable? With the exception of a few details it is true. Doesn't it indicate something defective in Father G's personality? Was he too timid to state his case before the bishop? Had he so little faith in the Church that he could not open his heart to the father of the priests in the diocese? The bishop after all received him warmly. Perhaps he was depressed? In any event, he could have written to the bishop if he found it difficult to talk to him. Was Father G right or wrong?

No, Father G was not suffering from a depression. As far as one could tell, he had no special psychological problems. Yes, the bishop had received him warmly. No, Father G was not timid. Yes, he could have written but he did not. The root question—is it possible to be a priest and a pastor at the same time?—was not a general one. Father G was talking about his own particular case.

Then why did he leave? A rational, perfectly logical explanation of his conduct would no doubt be desirable. We might like to see him, for example, as a saint confronting the monster of authoritarianism. Could Father G himself have given a rational explanation for his conduct? How many men lead perfectly rational lives?

We offer the following as a partial explanation. When Father G went to see the bishop, he had not yet decided to leave the priesthood. He merely wanted a different position. When he was talking to the bishop, or perhaps while he was waiting in the ante-chamber, it occurred to him that his deep feeling was "incommunicable." The bishop was kind and affable but did not suspect for a moment the drama that was being played out. One word perhaps would have been enough to determine a different outcome. But that word was not forthcoming. Father G withdrew into himself; he repressed his questions, his rebellion and his doubts. This was the beginning of a crisis—for when a man questions the whole direction of his life, there is always a serious crisis, in even the strongest and most resolute—which later became acute. Father G's visit to the bishop was a first step that led to his departure a few months later. He began by criticizing the parish structure and ended by judging the Church as a whole and deciding that he could be faithful to his vocation only by leaving the clergy.

For those unfamiliar with clerical circles, it may come as a surprise that communication between bishops and priests is so difficult. But this is precisely one of the major aspects of the present crisis of the priesthood which is, among other things, a crisis of authority and obedience. Despite certain real efforts on the part of some bishops, relationships between bishops and priests are for the most part nonexistent.

The bishops know this and since the Council have shown a desire to establish closer contacts. A speech by Bishop Gufflet of Limoges to his priests on annual retreat is one sign of this new mentality: "Please understand that from the bottom of my heart I wish to be your friend, the friend of each and every one of you. . . . Relations in friendship suppose relations in truth. . . . Because we are poor, I as well as you, it must be understood that there is no rule which says that we must say everything. The only rule is never to say the contrary of what we think. Not every truth need necessarily be spoken. If I have something to tell you and think that you are not ready to hear it, I shouldn't say it because of the friendship I have for you. Perhaps I could tell you in a month or in a year. And reciprocally, even though I am a bishop, I am not made of marble. If six or seven priests criticize me on the same day, how do you imagine I would feel in the evening? Have pity on me too. I ask only that if you have disagreeable things to tell me, tell me in friendship. For I am a man even though I am a bishop." [1]

At a meeting of European bishops in the Netherlands in July, 1967, Bishop Marty, vice-president for the French Episcopal Conference, noted that the idea of authority was evolving in the Church: "The final decisions at the diocesan level rest with the bishop but aided by dialogue with his priests and the laity." To illustrate his point, he cited the words of a young priest on the occasion of his recent ordination. To the ritual question, "Do you promise obedience and honor to myself and my successors?" the young priest answered, "Yes, I promise, but only in dialogue."

Other bishops throughout the world have likewise pointed out that the notions of authority and obedience are undergoing an evolution. For example, Cardinal Suenens of Belgium: "If we are adults, we do not have the right to obey otherwise than as adults. The superior has the last word but not the second last."

Nevertheless priests everywhere complain about their unsatisfactory relations with bishops.

In West Germany, the clergy complains that no one "at the top" is concerned with the individual priest. This was one of the conclusions of the survey undertaken by the bishops of the Rhineland to determine the causes of the vocation shortage. "The interviewers were surprised," the official report stated, "by the extent of resentment toward ecclesiastical authority on the part of young priests. They are in almost all cases in opposition to it."

In Spain a survey conducted by the religious journal *Pa-*

[1] Complete text in *Masses Ouvrières*, No. 240, May, 1967.

labra revealed that several hundred priests (from all dioceses) desired most of all "to have more contact with the bishop." In 1966, William Du Bay, of the Los Angeles diocese, was suspended by Cardinal McIntyre for trying to organize a priests' union. The fact that such an idea could suggest itself is indicative of the state of priest-bishop relationships.

In Latin America they speak of the "enormous abyss" between the high clergy on the one hand and the lower clergy and educated laity on the other. The situation in these countries is special since, with the exception of Mexico, there are close institutional ties between Church and state. Many countries, moreover, have never renounced the *patronato*, the ancient right of the Spanish crown to name bishops to its overseas colonies. Even where *patronato* is not formally invoked, the bishop knows that he owes his promotion to the president of the republic, who is usually a conservative or a reactionary. If he wants a new cathedral, he addresses himself to the civil authorities. The fear of communism binds him even more closely to the government and separates him from his priests—especially those who live in contact with the poor, dare to speak out against the existing social order, and reject the conservative monolithism which the bishop tries to impose upon them under threat of sanctions.

In France a survey of rural priests showed that 26 percent of those interviewed thought that all priests, or most of them at any rate, suffered from the bishop's lack of understanding.[2] Another survey (also among rural priests) indicated that not one priest out of five was satisfied with his relationship with his superior.[3] Pope Paul VI recognized this malaise when, on November 23, 1965, he received the Latin American bishops present at the Council and told them that their "very first

[2] Maître, *op. cit.*
[3] "Le clergé rural en France," *Lumière et vie,* January–April, 1966.

duty was to assist and comfort their priests." He also spoke
at some length about the paternity of bishops in his encyclical *Sacerdotalis Caelibatus:* "Before being the superiors and
judges of your priests, be their masters, their fathers and
friends, their good and kind brothers, always ready to understand, to sympathize, to help. In every possible way en-
courage your priests to be your personal friends and to be
very open with you. This will not weaken the relationship of
juridical obedience; rather it will transform it into pastoral
love, so that they will obey more willingly, sincerely and
securely" (No. 93).

Too late? Yes, a little. Priests have the feeling that they
were forgotten at the Council. "This Council will go down
in history as the Council of the episcopacy, not of the priesthood," Bishop Soares of Mozambique has said. Trent was the
Council of priests, Vatican I the Council of popes and Vatican II the council of the bishops. Must priests wait until the
wheel comes full circle with Vatican III?

There are many reasons for this revolt against authority.
Like celibacy, the bishop is in a sense a scapegoat. He is a
kind of "second mate." The Canadian psychoanalyst Eliott
Jacques has remarked that in the English navy everyone can
project their aggressiveness on the second mate, thus freeing
the captain for more important duties. To protect the highest
authority, the second mate bears all the discontent and criticism that would otherwise be inflicted on the leader. All
things being equal, a somewhat similar situation prevails in
the Church. The bishop plays second mate to the pope or,
more exactly, to the ecclesial institution. To protect the latter, the bishop is put in the defendant's box. But he is
scarcely comfortable there. Thus he fails to take an interest
in his priests, many of whom think that all problems would
be resolved if they had a bishop who was more intelligent,
more understanding, more inclined to dialogue. This attitude

is the more frequent the further away the bishop is. One hesitates to criticize oneself or close colleagues. The bishop is more removed, and we are inclined to project "evil" outside of us. Priests are not undergoing a crisis, in this view. The bishop is not what he should be.

This kind of behavior is often encountered in priests who are still to some extent infantile, which is to say aggressive. The adult is liberated from those aggressive reactions that are due to infantile reflexes. Sometimes the child is aggressive toward his father because he knows the latter will not use his real power against him. The priest sometimes acts the same way toward the Church and its representative in his eyes, the bishop or his delegate. Father X calls his former seminary superior an "imbecile," his vicar general "an opportunist," his dean "lusty," his pastor "a stuck-up runt," and his bishop a "hypocrite." Father Z, a weak personality who was pushed into the priesthood more or less against his will, is convinced that his bishop hates him.

These are characteristic attitudes. As a man living alone and at the same time a member of a strongly hierarchical body, the priest feels the need to be recognized and protected by the group, especially by authority. Such recognition gives him a sense of his own personal worth, something he, like every other human being, needs. Thus the priest is extremely sensitive to the attitude of authority toward him. More than the professional man, he feels the need of honest dialogue with his superiors because he is alone.

This is the psychological context. But we must also realize that there are objective reasons for this crisis. There is first of all the weight of the past. The bishop was once a feudal lord; in latter times he has become a highly placed executive. In both situations he has been distant from his priests. Something of that spirit subsists today.

The bishop remains a distant person. No one quite knows

what he does. How many priests would be able to describe a typical day in the life of their bishop? He is not always desirous of contact. Today, it is true, there is a new breed of bishops who are direct and friendly. These are the post-conciliar bishops. But other post-conciliar bishops remain reticent and aloof, rarely visiting their priests and then only for short periods. The clergy complains that they are misunderstood, that their bishop is unable to share their experience.

Formerly bishops were chosen because of their theology degrees or special studies they had taken, preferably at Rome. This is no longer necessarily the case. Administrators, for example, who have had the opportunity to make themselves known, furnish a good portion of the new bishops, but they are just as distant from the parish clergy.

From the moment he is nominated, the bishop must strive to overcome the prejudices, sometimes even the hostility, of his priests. Often he succeeds. Often he does not. In Paraguay the apostolic nuncio on his own initiative named Moleon Andreu, a man opposed to the spirit of Vatican II, as auxiliary bishop of Asuncion, the capital of the country. The archbishop himself did not seem to have been consulted. Most of the priests and religious of the country protested this appointment. This is becoming more and more possible in the post-conciliar Church. In increasing numbers priests and laity want to have some say in the nomination of their bishops.

Father Michonneau, one of the French pioneers of parish reform, has made this melancholy observation: if priests were allowed to choose their own diocese, many of the latter would be empty.

All of this has called forth episcopal denunciations in the old style. Many priests with new ideas have been silenced. But bishops who react in this fashion do not understand the urgency of what is being said. It is a veritable distress signal. Or, if they do understand, they rarely act like the fathers they are supposed to be. When a father hears his son cry out in pain, he does not tell him to be quiet. He tries to find out what is wrong.

But the Church, as a psychoanalyst has said, is "a society of connivance." In it whispering is preferred to confrontation, the half-truth to clarity. Everyone complains about this —the bishops because they are poorly informed, the priests because they are afraid to tell their bishops the truth and, when they do, feel obliged to excuse themselves beforehand. Everyone complains but nothing changes.

But let us not exaggerate. Disraeli's remark quoted earlier about hasty generalizations applies here. Some bishops live so simply that they win the admiration of their priests. Many more have become aware that the problem of their relations with the clergy is crucial. This in itself represents considerable progress. The Council stressed the necessity of a presbyterium, the union of bishops with their priests. Here and there diocesan councils have been organized, with representatives of the clergy meeting periodically with the bishop. We shall have to wait before judging how effective these are. But already there are signs of dissatisfaction. Archbishop Dwyer of Birmingham (England) told a meeting of European bishops that the consultative voice of the diocesan councils was like that of the British parliament four hundred years ago. Other such councils operate like registry offices. In any case, there are many traditions to overcome and the creation of a truly effective presbyterium will be a long process. As Father Rétif has remarked: "The flagrant lack of cooperation among priests in France and the conditions that cause this individualism makes the hope of a presbyterium in the spirit of the Council illusory for some time to come." [4]

[4] *Masses ouvrières*, No. 240, May, 1967.

Some bishops concerned with this problem have appointed handpicked priests to keep in contact with the clergy at large. But the clergy objects: "We are like the sons of a businessman who has no time to look after his own children and hires subalterns to do it."

In view of the seriousness of this crisis, priests are often accused of having lost the spirit of obedience. This is probably true. They are impregnated, as are we all, with the spirit of the modern world which does not consider obedience a major virtue but rather sees it as an alienation from human freedom and a refusal to take responsibilities. But every problem of obedience is a problem of authority and every crisis of obedience is also a crisis of authority.

Generations of priests in the past doubted less the content of faith than the effectiveness of pastoral methods. They felt it was not for them to seek out the truth. Their role was to obey, to do what they were told. Today priests want to understand before obeying. This doesn't mean that they will always obey once they have understood. And some refuse to understand. But any form of authoritarianism is intolerable for them.

Yet authoritarianism manifests itself frequently. It is common for priests to be shuffled from one parish to another, without being consulted and without knowing the reasons, like pawns on a chessboard. This happens routinely to assistants. Sometimes those more prestigiously placed suffer the same fate. For example, in 1967, Father William K. Leahy, one of the three American secretaries to the general secretariat of the Council was dismissed from his position as a seminary professor by order of the archbishop of Philadelphia. He was named an assistant in a small parish. This decision was taken, it seems, because of a speech Father Leahy had given on the Council and the necessity of *aggiornamento* in the Church. But will we ever know? The archbishop gave no reason or explanation for his action. In France, Father M entered the seminary after a brilliant college career. He found the atmosphere stifling but persevered until ordination, although by that time the spirit of rebellion was seething within him. He was named to a parish with one of those impossible pastors. He felt that his talents were being wasted and he went to see his bishop who told him, "I want to break your pride," and without further ado sent him to a remote parish in the country. Today the former Father M is a well-known sociologist and happy. Cases abound of priests being punished because they are considered "progressive."

Bishops want to be obeyed in the name of faith, faith in Christ, faith in the Church. Some justify their claim to obedience by quoting the Gospel: "Who hears you, hears me." All well and good. But this does not mean that everything they say comes from the mouth of God. It means that they must make every effort to make their words conform to the will of God, that they speak as Christ might have spoken.

But here is the paradox: this authoritarian attitude goes hand in hand with great permissiveness. Many laymen feel that priests run parishes any way they please. That is why to change parishes is always to enter an unknown world. Questions which torment the laity, like birth control, are answered in different ways. Some priests apply the directives of the magisterium strictly; others interpret them liberally; and so forth. The layman with "the right address" can get any answer he desires. This is because authority prefers to concern itself with secondary problems—unless, of course, it is altogether impotent—and let the essential work itself out.

The problem of authority is, therefore, an important factor in clerical defection.

Father D became a priest because he wanted to minister to the working classes. Because he was exceptionally gifted,

his superiors urged him, practically forced him, to go on to
higher studies in philosophy and theology. Father D was not
happy with the new direction his life had been given and he
let his superiors know this. They reacted in a classical manner by treating him as a malcontent who would have to be
taught humility. He was sent to a boarding school to teach
mathematics to high school students. This was the last straw.
Father D renounced the priesthood, frustrated in every way.
In secular life this kind of thing can happen. But there one
can always change jobs. Furthermore, the individual is protected from arbitrary manipulation by well-defined procedures. Father D could not change jobs. Finding his assignment
intolerable and unable to communicate with his bishop, he
had no choice but to leave the priesthood.

The former Father D has given a good deal of thought to
the problems of priests. "The Church," he says, "is an immense administrative machine. Everything is codified and
rigorously regimented. The laity, however, are somewhat
luckier than priests. With no constraint other than conscience
and without risking any sanction other than regret, the layman can transgress the Church's rules. In such cases there is
little that the Church can do. But priests have little choice
between obedience and the terrible alternative that is called
defection. They occupy an almost unique position in the
world today: most of their lives are controlled by the same
institution and the same person. The layman has more variety in his life—profession, family, recreational activities, and
so forth. And each of these activities is relatively autono-
mous. But everything is welded into a whole for priests. The
married man who is having trouble with his boss can go
home and forget about him. The priest is dependent on his
superior twenty-four hours a day, day in and day out. This
is hard to take."

Many priests develop a false love for this all-embracing

authority. In the seminary they were taught an obedience that is all too often indistinct from passivity. Thus they expect—especially today when everything is being called into question—authority to tell them what to do. "Let the bishop take his responsibilities seriously," they say. But the bishop has no easy recipes in his pocket. He himself, flanked as he usually is by advisers from the business world, is looking for answers. In the days when the priest had a canon law to apply to every situation and celebrated an immutable liturgy, it was easier for the bishop to dialogue with him. Today he is confronted with more fundamental questions: What should be done? How must one live? The superior's authority is not respected, and his authoritarianism is rejected outright unless it is accompanied by precise directives, clear and applicable orders of a nature to assuage the subordinate's insecurity.

6

The Case Against the Church

CHARLES DAVIS, the English theologian, wrote in A Question of Conscience that his decision to leave the priesthood and the Church was the result of years of theological research. He was convinced that Catholicism could not justify its claim to be the only true Church of Christ.

Early in 1967, James Kavanaugh, an angry young American priest, published a book entitled *A Modern Priest Looks at His Outdated Church*. A few months after publication it had sold 140,000 copies and Father Kavanaugh announced that he had asked his bishop to be reduced to the lay state. "I've had enough of beating my head against a brick wall," he said. He also explained that his defection should be understood as a protest against the failure of bishops to translate the spirit of Vatican II into action. On the same occasion he suggested that all the books of canon law be thrown into the Tiber. "All I want," he said, "is the freedom to find God without arrogant priests telling me that I am incapable." Kavanaugh married at the end of 1967 and is now a marriage counselor in La Jolla, California.

Neither a theologian nor the author of a best-seller, Father F, a former assistant in a French suburb, has a more complex attitude. "For the past two or three years," he explains, "the preoccupations of the Church have become more and more alien to me. Resounding declarations by the pope or bishops impress me less and less. In fact they don't interest me at all. They are so far removed from the real world, from the interests of the men and women I met in my parish. I took seriously what I had been taught—to go to the poor, the abandoned. I was in daily contact with unbelievers. I practically lived with them. It is perfectly clear to me that they inhabit a world that the Church is totally unsuited for. I grew weary of the whole situation. The passivity of practicing Christians—how many sermons I preached on that theme!—the reluctance to undertake reforms that everyone agrees are necessary, all of this influenced my decision." Still Father F adds: "I always feel responsible for the Church and the world. In my small way, of course." He left the clergy with serious reservations about the Church but he still considers himself a member of the Church.

Publicly or not, and for various reasons, the Church is

literally on trial today. A psychiatrist who does a good deal of work with troubled priests observes: "This is something new. Today many Catholics are questioning the structure of the Church in a non-neurotic fashion. Formerly, this sort of thing was usually a symptom of adolescent rebellion. That is no longer the case." This critical atmosphere causes or facilitates many defections from the clergy.

It might seem surprising to some that such criticism of the Church should take place at a time when the Church seems to have given proof through the Council of her capacity for reform and inner dynamism. But there is a psycho-sociological explanation for this apparent paradox. When a community that has long been governed by an authoritarian regime reforms, liberal voices tend to become strident. The leader who gradually tries to liberalize an authoritarian regime has many more problems than the dictator who preceded him. He must face up to the critics. And if he lets them have their way, they will go to even further extremes to test his liberalism.

The Council is the principal cause of this criticism of the Church. Some Catholics didn't think the Council went far enough. As some armies are always late for war, so the Church will always be in arrears of a Council. This opinion was put forth on a BBC program in London on September 14, 1966: "Vatican II attacked a number of problems that arose in the fifteenth century which the Church could not resolve in the sixteenth century. The work of Vatican II also belatedly remedied certain other problems inherited from the eighteenth, nineteenth and early twentieth centuries."

For others the spirit of the Council is not being translated into action quickly enough. Vatican II seemed to them to be a new departure. But the hierarchical Church apparently regards it more as a point of arrival so as not to shock the sensibilities or unsettle the habits of the masses of conservative Catholics.

The criticisms of the impatient are familiar. The Church, they say, is always a prisoner of its outdated structures. It is too institutional, not prophetic enough. The Roman Curia, at least up until the recent reforms, is readily denounced as a hotbed of reactionaries, indeed fascists. (The secrets of another age which shroud the Vatican's method of making decisions no doubt makes the Curial officials seem more redoutable and Machiavellian than they really are.) The Church's system of government seems obsolete, ineffective and foreign to the spirit of the Gospels. These criticisms are particularly loud in Anglo-Saxon countries where opposition to Roman centralism comes naturally. At the end of 1967, thirty-two canon lawyers meeting in New York typically requested the introduction of certain "constitutional principles" into the Church's code in order "to limit the powers of those in authority." They called for a more equitable distribution of power between the pope and bishops and separation of the legislative, executive and judiciary functions as a step toward greater protection of individual rights.

Other critics are more disturbed by the apparent wealth of the Church and the secrecy that surrounds its bookkeeping system (unlike state budgets which are made public) and also by the ridiculous display of pomp under the pretext of worshiping God (aren't these men in purple and fine lace, in ermine and mitres, really worshiping themselves?) or, even worse, on the grounds that the good people "like this sort of thing" (they also like circuses and chorus lines). Still others, less concerned with reform at the top, are more worried about adapting the basic structures. They note, for example, that the present parish structure is inadequate but that no serious study of other possible ways of regrouping the Christian community have been undertaken and that missionary priorities, which are poorly defined, are not taken seriously enough by the Church.

The hierarchical Church's complicity with worldly powers is becoming less and less tolerable. Bernanos denounced this many years ago: "The Church compromises herself as little as possible with poor sinners. She avoids embarrassing governments like the plague. True, she offers admirable definitions of oppression but her irreproachable definitions, which delight the philosophers, are of no great help to the oppressed since they almost always fail to name the oppressors."[1] Many think that this judgment, despite some recent minor ameliorations, has lost nothing of its actuality. A survey in the diocese of Santiago (Chile) invited "all men of goodwill" to express their feelings about the Church. A large majority of those who responded felt that the Church was more a political and economic power than a community of brothers reflecting the presence of Christ. "The Church," Cardinal Silva Henriquez concluded, "must devote less time to formal and institutional pursuits and become more fraternal, poorer, more solidary."

The image that the hierarchical Church presents to the world is blurred and deformed. In Lima, Cardinal Landazuri interrupted work on his cathedral and gave the allocated funds to the poor. On the other hand, Cardinal Jaime de Barros Camara of Río de Janeiro built an immense cathedral in the heart of the city where there were already some twenty other churches, all of them practically useless since the population center had long since shifted to the suburbs. Paul VI's periodic gestures on behalf of the poor and disinherited cannot be taken seriously unless he takes the powerful to task—which he rarely does and then only with the greatest circumspection. On the contrary, such gestures to-

[1] G. Bernanos, *Chemin de la croix des ames.*

ward the poor are considered demogogic. Some Spanish
Catholics participate in strikes and go to jail, but this is
counterbalanced by the "landed clergy" who reap the profits
of their possessions with little concern for the welfare of the
peasants who cultivate them. Bishop Helder Camara won
world-wide admiration for his vigorous criticism of selfish
property owners, but in 1965 two Brazilian bishops published
a brochure in which they affirmed that "Catholics who benefit by agrarian reform are morally guilty of theft." Paul VI
intervened in favor of peace in Vietnam, but Cardinal Spell-
man could take an almost opposite stand without being disavowed. Everyone knows of countries where the hierarchical
Church is still, despite certain timid efforts of reform, the best
supporter of regimes whose principal concerns are neither
social justice nor individual rights.

It appears as though the Church is reluctant to break with
her ancient alignments. She is consequently forced to equi-
vocate, to run with the hares and hunt with the hounds, and
ends by dancing to the world's tune. Thus she cannot say
with Christ: "The spirit of the Lord is upon me. Wherefore
he hath annointed me to preach the gospel to the poor: he
hath sent me to heal the contrite of heart, to preach deliver-
ance to the captives and sight to the blind, to set at liberty
them that are bruised, to preach the acceptable year of the
Lord and the day of reward" (Luke 4:18). She has not yet
quite decided upon her image.

And the world which began to listen to the Church once
again is wondering whether or not it erred.

A few years ago the relations between the Church and the
world seemed promising. The era of John XXIII opened a
path of hope, less at the level of reforms and decisions (some
were important, others disappointing) than in terms of an
attitude. The Church advanced boldly in a spirit of discovery, without fear of blows or pitfalls—and the world began

to love her. The pope scarcely left Rome, but the world seemed willing to go to him. Now the Church has reverted to an attitude of suspicion. She has fallen back into the old habits. She has drawn up her defenses on all sides. She is too cunning. But the world instinctively distrusts a Church that is too cunning. She may well create new commissions to study this or that, secretariats for unbelievers, Buddhists, Jews or what have you and increase summit meetings with important and representative personages. But this will not make men listen. The world will pay attention to the Church only when she is disarmed and simple. The image and destiny of a Church that is loved only when her attitude is evangelical in conformity with the mind of her founder is a worthy theme for meditation.

The Church as it is now proclaims that "we must go to the poor" but remains all too often with the rich. She is like an operatic chorus that sings "let us go forward" but never moves. Similarly when she speaks of openness to the world and presents herself as the servant of the world and men. Henry H, a former priest, says the Church "flirts with the world without really espousing its fate. She reneges on her word whenever it suits her." Father Yves Congar agrees that the Church has not succeeded in convincing the world of her good faith. "Many nonbelievers detect a tactical maneuver in this pretended conversion to man. They suspect that the Church is playing this card simply because her ancient claims to power are no longer effective. . . . The Church must make her offer to serve man and the world *credible* in terms of their success rather than her own." [2]

There is a minority among both the "integralists" and the "progressives" who fear that the Church will be too well accepted by the world. In an affluent society such a Church would ask no questions. She would make few demands.

[2] "Nouveau monde et parole de Dieu," *Esprit,* October, 1967.

She would no longer dare speak of poverty. She would be fashionable but not controversial, satisfying certain vague needs of religiosity. This danger was very clearly seen by Jean-Marie Domenach, the editor of *Esprit:*

I am among those who have called for a certain *rapprochement,* if not a reconciliation (that is a nasty word), between the Church and the world. But I took this position some twenty years ago. The Church then was undergoing a period of renewal with the worker-priest movement, and we faced a fairly consistent and stable world that had its values, its ideologies, its beliefs, its philosophies of history. Today it is a contrary situation. We are confronted with a world which has been emptied of beliefs and ideas. Even atheists have lost their virulence. Catholics used to baptize barbarian civilizations (this is obviously a very general and unqualified statement). What can they baptize today? There is no longer anything to baptize. . . . We are calling for a modernization of the Church, for a *rapprochement* between the Christian faith and the modern world. Yet that world seems to be vanishing. Wouldn't such a reconciliation in reality be a kind of compromise with this world's lack of values, its indifference, its generalized euphoria? If reconciliation between the Church and the modern world took place at this level, let us say at the level of a Camus-like moralism, if religion becomes a function of public relations, a way of fitting people into life, we would achieve just the opposite of what men like myself dreamed about when we called for reconciliation between the Church and the modern world some twenty years ago.[3]

The danger of a lack of openness to the world and the danger of too close an identification with that world are inextricably bound up with each other, and often enough the same persons denounce both dangers.

These discussions and criticisms are not new. They were being aired long before the Council, at least in some countries. Vatican II merely provided a point of reference as well as new impetus. But Vatican II has also created a new situation, a new attitude on the part of certain Catholics which we might call indifference, a lack of interest in the hierarchical Church, the ecclesial institution. This indifference also

[3] *Panorama Chrétien,* February, 1966.

exists among priests and is an important reason why many of them are unhappy or leave.

The Council in effect made change worthwhile. Theologians who were put on the index and sanctioned ten years earlier were honored and listened to at Vatican II and even quoted in the encyclicals. Regulations that had been imposed upon generations of Catholics were suddenly outdated. This caused serious crises. The confusion on the whole question of birth control is significant in this respect. As one layman put it: "The matter is not as simple as we were once assured it was. Many Catholic homes have been forced to rethink this question since apparently the pope himself doesn't know what decision to take." [4] The notion of change necessarily implies that of relativity. Since the rules of yesterday do not hold today, nothing leads us to believe that those of today will hold tomorrow. What is now prohibited will perhaps one day be permitted or even praised, or perhaps, rejected.

When regulations are provisory, no one wants them imposed by an external authority. If this authority insists upon maintaining its power, many will leave the community rather than submit to it. And many laymen and priests look upon Rome and even the local Church structure as an external authority. This is because, it is said, they lack a sense of the Church. Perhaps. But this accusation doesn't solve the problem. In fact these men and women consider themselves members of the people of God. Because they have no access to the centers of decision and no knowledge of the mechanism of decision-making, they question their relationship to authority. A transitory law cannot be tolerated by all the members of a community unless it emanates from that community and is accepted by it. For example, we could imagine the members of a community agreeing to do this or that in light of their present mentality and the state of scholarship.

[4] A comment made prior to *Humanae Vitae.*—B.M.

Such an attitude is quite compatible with the existence of a revelation which must constantly be deepened and to which reference must always be made in defining new modes of thought and methods of action.

But this is not the mind of the Roman Catholic Church today. Consequently, increasing numbers of laymen and priests in practice ignore her authority, which means leaving the priesthood for many priests. Their attitude has been well described by François Roustang in an article in the Jesuit review *Christus* entitled, "The Third Man." Its impact was so great that "the third man" is a commonly accepted expression to define this mentality.

As a result of the profound and rapid changes in the Church, Roustang argues, many Catholics have acquired a personal liberty that has estranged them from their backgrounds, whether conservative or reformist. "A third race, a third people, a third man is emerging and there is some danger that he will be ignored." Such Christians sharply distinguish between faith in God and in Jesus Christ from faith in the Church as it is expressed in the liturgy and the official positions of the hierarchy.

In the past everything hung together. Although this or that teaching might have been critically received, there was never any doubt that the teachings of Christ and the Church were in fact identical. But the critical spirit ushered in by Vatican II, the Church's confession of past faults and the questioning of certain practices and laws affected the very principle of the Christ-Church identification. Now the connection between the two is less clear. It seems dangerous and even wrong to take what the Church affirms today as an absolute since her past affirmations have proven inadequate and in some cases have been contradicted. Consequently the Christian must rely on his own conscience. If the teaching Church formulates new regulations, he may accept them as guide lines but he can never take them as Gospel truth. He knows that the desire for reform begun in the Council now depends on him and will be furthered by his own efforts to achieve lucidity. . . . We now see, although most often we deplore it, that the vigor of the conciliar debates set off a movement of freedom of speech and thought in the Church which, far from rejecting the faith, scrutinizes its foundations and rejects all sclerosis.

These Catholics are also aware that the new liberty they have acquired enables them to encounter others in a deeper spirit of fraternity.

Their faith is not in question. Since they are now guided more by their consciences than by rules, they have a clearer notion of what the demands of faith are. That is why they call for a "new kind of relationship between faith and the law."

"If we are not careful and refuse to acknowledge the evidence," Roustang concludes, "the indifference toward the Church which is already widespread will become more pronounced. It will not as in the past take the form of open conflict or abandon; rather it will manifest itself as a giant disinterest toward that mountain of efforts which untiringly brings forth mice. The rejection of the old system may even be justified in the name of that faith which the Council helped these Christians rediscover and live more deeply."

It is no doubt possible to interpret this as an indication of modern man's inclination to make his conscience the unique norm of decision-making and conduct, his tendency to determine the meaning of life by himself. Still, the men and women who have adopted it are the very ones who insist on the importance of community in contemporary society and they are often members of dynamic communities themselves.

These communities are relatively numerous in a country like the United States where they speak of an "underground Church." It is comprised of more or less clandestine groups, including priests and religious, which live on the margin of the official institutions of the Church and celebrate the Eucharist with little regard for established forms. The members of these communities reproach the Church for its timidity in implementing post-conciliar renewal and the lack of effective commitment on such questions as the struggle for peace and Negro rights. In an article published in the *National Catholic Reporter,* Donald Thorman cites as a typical example the case of a young woman who belonged to an active civil rights organization. The Council awakened great hopes in her. But disappointment soon set in. She went to live with a friend in a poor sector of the city, motivated by a desire to serve. On her first visit to the local parish, the pastor advised her to discontinue her plans and offered her a position in a parochial organization. She never went back, but joined a secular group instead.

We encounter this kind of phenomenon more often today, in Europe as well as in America. Thus it is not merely a question of people wanting an individualistic faith. What is rejected is not the community as such. It is the Church as a monarchical and aristocratic institution imposing laws that individual conscience cannnot accept.

It is likely that this attitude will become commonplace in years to come. Today it is one of the most recent and most fundamental causes of clerical defection.

The criticisms directed against the Church call, however, for several comments.

1. There is a good deal of confusion about the very nature of the Church. For some progressive thinkers, it is identical with the human race. For most, it is the hierarchy and especially Rome. Others adopt the definition given by the Council.

Most criticism today is directed toward the hierarchical aspect of the Church. This is undoubtedly an error although a natural one. Rome and the hierarchy have for so long spoken for the whole Church that confusion has resulted. The best of Council texts will change nothing unless the experience of the Church is lived in a new way.

2. Are the critics of the Church-as-an-institution against a few obvious deficiences in the way it functions or are they hostile to institutions as such, to all instruments of collective action? Some draw a sharp distinction between the way the ecclesial structures work and the ecclesial structures themselves. Thus the priest who had faith in the Church and precisely in the name of this faith contested the attitude of the authorities and the fact that the clerical society had to be organized on the model of the old regime. He chose to leave, as he said, "in order to raise the problem."

But not everyone makes this distinction. There are those, in Holland for example, who not only reject the Church as a special kind of institution but reject practically all ecclesial institutions. The process of secularization that began with modern times, they argue, has made the distinction between the sacred and the profane irrelevant. Religion has ceased to represent a specific domain. It is becoming primarily an evangelical ethic, inspiring men and women whose duty it is to bear witness to the values of Christianity in their social activities. Under these conditions the ecclesial institution loses all *raison d'être*. But a Church that is so identified with the world and so deprived of any distinguishing characteristics will in practice cease to exist. Which raises the question: "In stripping the Church of everything that identifies it as a society, might we not compromise our mandate to propagate the Word of God?" [5]

It seems unlikely that the faith can be lived without an institutional body, especially by the poor, the abandoned, and even the average man. It is even more unlikely that a community of faith could express itself and survive without such a body. On the other hand, it is true that every institu-

[5] René Remond, president of the Catholic Center of French Intellectuals, in *Esprit, op. cit.*

tion is a hardening of the *élan vital* that gave birth to it. How do we resolve this dilemma?

History indicates the necessity of the institutional Church to transmit the message of Christ. This was expressed in the words of a young convert: "For twenty centuries that institution which is called the Church has conserved the evangelical text in all of its authenticity. The Church, by virtue of an incarnation that is tenacious, durable, tormented and suffering, has delivered to us the good news which is truly that of the Incarnation. She has the right to our help and our friendship." [6]

Father Henri de Lubac, in a long meditation in which he quotes Teilhard de Chardin, also celebrates the Church's vitality: "At a time when many are as though hypnotized by the signs of old age in the Church, the more discerning eye of love leads me to discover in her hidden forces and silent activities which make her perpetually young. Great things are born in her heart and contagiously convert the world." [7]

Others base their argument on the authority of Christ. "The great justification of the Church is that she is the Church of Christ, the Church which Christ founded." [8]

This argument cuts little ice with the critics of the Church. They do not deny that Christ founded the Church but they point out that Christ did not give her the institutional form that is now under criticism.

This is a painful and complicated controversy. For obvious reasons we can do no more than touch upon it in this book. Let us note, however, that to recognize that the Church is indispensable does not exclude the necessity of far-reaching

[6] Georges Hourdin, "Qu'est-ce donc l'Eglise?" *Informations catholiques internationales*, July 1, 1967.
[7] In *Civitas*, Lucerne.
[8] Jacques Leclerc, "Aimer l'Eglise," *Choisir*, June, 1967.

reforms. She must show herself more humble, less mono-
lithic, and rid herself of all authoritarianism.

And she is far from having done this.

3. Some of the criticisms directed against the Church are
motivated by impatience. There are those who shout, "Faster,
faster," while others caution: "Wait. There are 500,000,000
Catholics. They must first digest the Council before we go
any further. You cannot turn a transatlantic liner as easily
as a small fishing boat. It takes time and space."

This argument has some value. A minimum of cohesion is
necessary for any community. However, to want everyone
to march to the same tune is unreasonable. The example of
liturgical renewal—still the only concrete manifestation of
conciliar reform for many Catholics—shows that the Catholic
people, despite a certain reluctance, can adapt to new
orientations easily enough. Of course, they complain when
progressives introduce a series of partial changes instead of
going directly to the heart of the matter in the first place.
This gives them the impression that they are entering a
period of perpetual change. As Péguy once wrote: "Against
a fully traditional situation, there is no better weapon than
a fully revolutionary situation."

The reformist argument for progress, moreover, would be
more widely accepted if it were supplemented by a massive
effort to educate the people. Otherwise, renewal often seems
like a laborious attempt to justify the real reasons why there
is so little of it: conservatism, fear of the future, prudence,
and so forth.

4. In much criticism of the Church there is an element of
aristocratic and disincarnate purism, a certain note of aggressiveness. In the past the Church was always ready to
blame others for her own faults and is still tempted to do so.
Today some Christians are giving her a taste of her own
medicine, thus practicing what Bishop Charrière of Geneva

calls "triumphalism in reverse." To seek an impossible purity and manifest superiority by abstracting oneself from the human community is an attitude that churchmen have often recommended to Christians. Again, there are those today who are turning this advice against the Church. They leave her in order to find "a pure and hard" Christianity. Perhaps we might say of them what Péguy said of Kant and his disciples: "Their hands are clean but they have no hands."

It is surprising to meet priests who seem to have only recently discovered the human side of the Church. Haven't they heard of the Inquisition, Alexander VI (the lover of Vannozza Catanei and Giulia Farnese and an advocate of political wars) or Julius II, also a political pope, who sold indulgences to raise funds for his construction program?

An aggressive attitude toward the Church is sometimes so infantile that one wonders whether some critics (both clerical and lay) will ever be satisfied as long as there is some barrier to overthrow or some law to declare outdated. This attitude is well summed up in the following quip: "If they succeed in getting the law of celibacy rescinded, they will probably want the right to practice polygamy."

5. Should one leave the Church in order to reform it? This question was widely discussed when Charles Davis left the Church. Hans Küng, who is about the same age as Davis, knew him well and defended him against unjust accusations. But he disapproved of his decision to leave the Church, arguing metaphorically that when the bark of Peter is caught in rough waters loyalty demands that we all row together.

Archbishop Roberts, formerly of Bombay and one who suffered greatly at the hands of the Holy Office, also opines that "one cannot help a ship in difficulty by deserting it." [9]

"I believe," he said, "that it is God's will for us to stay in

[9] Radio program entitled "800 million Christians," Radio-Luxembourg, March 19, 1967.

the Church, that it is His Church. I have always believed that the great majority of the human race will be saved in the Church. Christianity has only begun. Having lived a long time in the Orient, I have the greatest admiration for the pagan religions I encountered there. I have no difficulty in admitting that they are in many ways superior to Christianity. Gandhi, for example, understood the spirit of Christ better than most Christians. . . . But when one has received Christ from the Church, we cannot leave her. Nor can we separate the Church from the new meaning given it by Vatican II. She is the Body of Christ, known to millions and millions of people who are not known to us. For those of us who are members of the visible Church, it is God's will that we remain in it. There are many improvements to be made in the ship. But they can only be made from within."

Charles Davis addressed himself to this objection on the same program. "I think it is necessary to understand very clearly what we mean by the Church. If we understand it in its deepest sense, I do not see how it can be identified with the structure of the Roman Church. Those who believe in the Roman Church should seek their freedom in it. But that would be impossible for me unless the present structures were changed, because there is no place in them for freedom. It does not seem to me that the presence of Christ in the world today and the manifestation of that presence can be confined to the limits of the Roman Church. I think of the Christians I know, Christians who have a serious commitment to Christ. And I ask myself: are they inspired by the official Churches? I think not. Some are inspired by the Bible. Others find strength in the sacraments. But on the whole the structures of the official Church in fact constitute an obstacle to a full Christian life and do not represent a common faith and action."

In effect, Davis was asking where the true Church of

Christ is to be found. To criticize the Roman Church is at the same time to raise a question about the Church of Christ.

6. Critics of the Church sometimes reflect a crisis of faith in Christ. We frequently hear the accusation that they attack the Church because they don't believe in Christ. Who believes in Christ believes in the Church! This is no doubt true of some. But our preceding remarks show that it is only the structure of the Roman Church that is under attack. We must, therefore, ignore unfounded accusations. Moreover, we are not in possession of any techniques that could reliably measure the faith of others. That there is a crisis of faith among Catholics (priests and laity) is evident. When everything that humanly sustained the faith (habits of thought, the experience of prayer, and so forth) collapses, when the human conditions of faith are purified, when we become aware that our former faith was infantile and its motives impure, a terrible disillusionment sets in. We are tempted to throw the baby out with the bath water. But this crisis of faith cannot of itself account for the criticisms made of the Church, because in many cases they are motivated by faith in Christ. That this faith may weaken later on without the support of the Church is another question. In former times priests left the ministry because they lost the faith. That still happens occasionally. Most priests who leave today, however, seem to remain believers even though they are critical of the Church.

They are critical because they think that the Church is in a pre-Exodus state, attached to the bland certitudes of Egypt and hesitant to set forth across the desert to the land of freedom. Some urge her to begin this journey forthwith. Others have already departed, alone. They look upon themselves as an avant-garde patrol. But might they not be in reality lost children?

APPENDIX

A Dossier on Priests Who Leave

AN INVESTIGATION of the reasons why priests leave was necessary to the purposes of this book. We shall now assess this phenomenon and inquire into the situation of former priests, which is not always a fortunate one.

THE NUMBER OF DEPARTURES

The number of priests who leave (both secular and religious) is a closely kept secret at all levels. Church authorities are not inclined to discuss what they consider failures. But their attitude in fact has the opposite of the intended effect and leads the public to overestimate the number of departures.

Of course, they couldn't give reliable statistics even if they wanted to—except at the diocesan level or in the case of those who have been officially laicized. Rome has no idea of the exact number of priests living in the world. The fantastic figures the Vatican releases each year is sufficient proof of this.

The same is true at the national level. The Church has traditionally been organized in terms of diocesan rather than national units. We now know how many priests there are in France, thanks to the work of the Reverend Julien Potel who, at the episcopacy's request, undertook a detailed demographic study of the secular clergy.[1] Still, Father Potel was forced to acknowledge that he could find no "complete or trustworthy statistics" on how many priests leave.

Some try to determine the number of departures by comparing the *Ordos* (which list all the priests in a given diocese) from year to year. But this method is not too reliable. Sometimes the *Ordos* list priests "on leave" or "on special assignment" who have as a matter of fact long since left.

Given the lack of statistics, we can only hope to provide a reasonably accurate estimate.

On a world scale there is no doubt that the number of departures has risen in the past few years. The Institute for Sacerdotal Assistance meeting in Lucerne noted that the number of those who leave the ministry "is increasing."

After the publication of Paul VI's encyclical on celibacy, Bishop Garolafo, a consultor to the Congregation of Faith, held a press conference in Rome. He was asked to comment upon the rumor that 10,000 petitions for dispensations from celibacy had been received by the Vatican in the past few years. The prelate answered that 4,000 dispensations had been requested between 1944 and 1966. Ninety percent of these, he added, were from older priests who wanted to regularize their situation [2] and 10 percent from young priests. These figures apparently did not include petitions for reduction to the lay state without dispensation from celibacy and obviously did not include those who left informally (and their numbers are increasing.) The global figure for these years is certainly higher than 4,000.

The press frequently suggests that the rate of defection is about 10 percent. Typically, the basis of this calculation is never mentioned. What it seems to mean is that the total

[1] Published as *Le clergé français* (Paris, Editions du Centurion).
[2] During Paul VI's pontificate Rome is more lenient. It is also true that a number of priests who have been out of the ministry for years have profited by the new spirit to regularize their situation.

number of priests who leave is one-tenth of the total clerical population at any given time. This would seem somewhat high for the current situation, at least in most countries.

In France a secret survey was conducted by Canon Boulard, one of the pioneers in religious sociology, at the request of the bishops. He determined the exact number of departures among the regular clergy in twenty-one dioceses for the period 1900–62. On this basis he projected an estimate for the country as a whole. For the years studied, he found that between 1,200 and 1,500 priests had left the ministry. This would indicate that the rate of defection is no more than 3 percent. We have no reliable statistics for the period after 1962 but there is evidence that departures have increased.

Canon Boulard's survey points up several facts:

1. The curve of clerical defection corresponds to periods of crisis: 1905 (the separation of Church and state, the modernist crisis); 1918–20 (a number of priests who found satisfaction in the army, where they could be "men among men," did not return to their dioceses after the war); 1945–55 (a similar situation after World War II, the appeal of Marxism, the crisis of the worker-priest movement).

2. The number of departures varies from diocese to diocese. It is difficult to determine the reasons for this. No doubt traditional Christian regions where the people exert strong pressure on the priest is a factor. Another factor is the quality of the bishops and diocesan leaders.

3. There is a discernible pattern of "chain departures." In a given city there may be twenty departures in one year and none for the next twenty years. It seems that some departures are "pre-arranged," also that one encourages others.

4. Almost all priests who leave were ordained young (at

twenty-two or twenty-three). Conversely, departures are rare among late vocations, less than one percent.

The recent upsurge of departures seems to have affected France less than other countries.

In the United States, with some 57,000 priests, more than 400 are reported to have left the ministry between June, 1966 and December, 1967. The total number of former priests (referred to as FP's) is said to be close to 5,000. In his book *Priestly Celibacy and Maturity*,[3] Father David O'Neill of New Zealand reports that while he was in the United States he repeatedly heard from diocesan authorities that the number of priests who leave is probably about 10 percent of the total. On this basis, we could estimate about 5,600 FP's for the year 1965. Father O'Neill noted that in his own country, where the ties between the priest and community are very close, the average would be less than 5 percent.

In Canada, departures have appreciably increased since the end of the Council. The press there follows the 10 percent yardstick and estimates that there are 1,600 former priests in the country, although these figures are disputed by Bishop Paul Grégoire of Montreal. In the last five years, he said, of the 923 secular priests in his diocese only 10 had asked to be dispensed, either temporarily or definitively. Of course, this argument does not take into consideration those who left without asking for dispensations. A more serious estimate was published by the Jesuit Review, *Relations* (February, 1967) by Father Gérard Hebert. He concluded that about 50 priests of the Montreal diocese left in 1965 and 1966. The crisis seems to have particularly affected the Jesuits. In the five years from 1961 to 1966, 75 of them left the company (two priests joined the diocese, 13 others and 60 scholastics who had taken vows returned to lay life). The

[3] New York, Sheed and Ward, 1965.

crisis was especially serious in Quebec because of the liberal
winds of Vatican II and the evolution of a province that had
long been a bastion of social and religious conservatism. The
explosion there, logically enough, was more keenly felt than
elsewhere.

An analogous situation presents itself among the Jesuits
in Latin America. In Argentina some 20 Jesuits left the order
in 1965. All of them had received a strict and authoritarian
formation.

The departure rate of both secular and regular clergy in
Chili, Colombia, Argentina and Brazil has also risen. Several
hundred priests have left in these countries since the Council
—not the mountain pastors who live in concubinage but
relatively important figures like vicar generals, seminary professors, and so forth who are opposed to the episcopacy because of its complicity with an oppressive capitalist regime.
At Mendoza in Argentina, Rome appointed a bishop whom
the priests did not want. As a result most of the leaders of
the diocesan clergy left, including Camilo Torres. Forced to
choose between the traditional structures of the Church and
service to their people, priests in growing numbers are
choosing the people.

In Europe statistics are difficult to come by. But the following is a fair estimate. In England the number of departures has increased in the recent past. Likewise in Holland.
According to the Pastoral Institute of the Netherlands in
Rotterdam, 60 priests (42 of them religious) left in 1966,
including a number of important and well-known figures.
In Belgium some 60 priests are reported to have married in
the same year. In France defections seem to have taken place
primarily among high school teachers who could not recon-
cile the priesthood (with all of its frustrations) and a lifelong
fate of teaching geography or mathematics. The situation
in Germany is somewhat like that of France. Partial sur-

veys indicate a recent rise in departures. Thirty were reported in the diocese of Fribourg alone in 1966. In Italy
there are many more departures than in France although
reports to the effect that 10,000 priests and religious have
returned to the lay state are obviously unrealistic. A strong
movement in favor of a married clergy has developed in
recent years. The journal *Europeo* regularly publishes "open
letters" from priests expressing their dissatisfaction and intentions to marry. The high rate of departures in that country can also be explained by a very traditional seminary
system that educates candidates in a vacuum and by the
methods of recruitment, especially in religious orders in
which the habit is worn by very young children (usually
recruited from poor families who cannot afford to educate
them).

To give a fair picture we should mention that many former priests do as a matter of fact return to the clergy. In
former times severe penances were imposed upon them.
Today it is much easier to return, although not many more
do. In *Sacerdotalis Caelibatus,* Paul VI affirms that "many
priests who for a time had been unfaithful to their obligations have, with the grace of the High Priest, found again
the path, and have given joy to all by becoming anew exemplary pastors" (No. 90).

This would appear to be an optimistic assessment of the
matter.

THE CHURCH'S ATTITUDE TOWARD THOSE WHO LEAVE

1. *Canon Law*

Canon law provides for reduction to the lay state. Laicization does not deprive the priest of the indelible character
of orders or the powers which he received, although to

exercise these powers would be "gravely illicit." The cleric who returns to the lay state "loses all rights and privileges." If he is a priest, he remains bound by the law of celibacy, except in those cases in which holy orders were received under external constraint. Then the Church judges that he is not bound by the responsibilities of ordination, including the obligations of the breviary and celibacy.

The Church disposes of several sanctions against priests who are in irregular situations, notably:

1. Suspension *a divinis* which prohibits the priest from any exercise of the power of orders (although he remains a priest).

2. Degradation, accompanied by reduction to the lay state. An exceptional procedure, degradation is pronounced by a tribunal of five judges. It is aimed against those who have already been suspended and continue "for a year to give grave scandal," or against those who have publicly joined a non-Catholic sect, have been found guilty of acts of violence against the pope or of homicide or have persevered in a civil marriage.

Other procedures are provided for in the case of religious. The most common of these is exclaustration. This provisory measure permits the religious to live a certain time in the world—for reasons of health, aiding his family and also to reflect on his future. Those who are exclaustrated are bound by their vows, and if they are priests, remain so. They must not, however, wear the habit and are no longer subject to their superiors but rather to the bishop of the diocese in which they reside. The religious with perpetual vows who leaves a religous house without the intention to return is considered an apostate and can be excommunicated. Finally, a religious can be "dismissed" if he publicly renounces the Catholic faith, if he "runs away" with a person of the op-posite sex and "attempts or contracts a marriage, even a civil marriage." If the "dismissed" religious is a priest, he is not reduced to the lay state but is "suspended."

So much for canon law. It is harsh and even its vocabularly smacks of anachronism. This is particularly true of the expression "reduction to the lay state" which evokes an age when laymen were considered second-order Catholics. The word derives from the Latin *reducere*, which mean "to lead back." Thus the word "reduction" is a mistaken translation, a rather unfortunate one which no one seems in any great hurry to correct.

The system has been liberalized somewhat during Paul VI's reign. In the early 1950's it was impossible for a priest to be released from his vow of celibacy even though he were laicized. Too, the formalities of laicization took a considerable period of time. Today it is accorded more readily, as is the dispensation from celibacy. Paul VI explains this in *Sacerdotalis Caelibatus*: "We have, in cases concerning ordination to the priesthood, been prepared to allow inquiry to extend beyond the provisions of the present canon law to other very grave reasons that give grounds for really solid doubts regarding the full freedom and responsibility of the candidate for the priesthood and his fitness for the priestly state. This has been done to free those who, on careful juridical consideration, of their case, are seen to be really unsuited" (No. 84). In many dioceses, moreover, bishops show greater understanding toward priests who wish to leave and expedite the formalities.

These modifications do not quite disarm the critics of the system. Reduction to the lay state without a dispensation from celibacy (happily becoming rarer) creates a situation in which it is difficult to define a person juridically. He is neither altogether a layman nor a priest and is deprived of the rights of both states. One of the few examples of a "pariah" still existing in the Western world is a Catholic phenomenon: the laicized priest who is bound by celibacy and, in certain countries where a concordat is in effect, cannot marry civilly. Should he appeal to international organizations because his human rights are violated?

"Many priests," notes a psychiatrist with refrence to reduction to the lay state, "resent this measure even when they have asked for it, because it seems to exclude them. They feel they are rejected, not from the clerical society but from the Church. This provokes some to aggressiveness. They wish to punish the clerical society as well as themselves and some create a scandal for precisely this reason, even going so far as to become beggars."

The pope himself, in the encyclical text cited above, implicitly recognizes the necessity for revising canon law on this point.

2. Material Assistance

When a priest leaves the clergy, he generally finds himself in a difficult material situation. In most cases he has little money and has trouble finding employment.

Many critics protest the fact that the Church lets men who have worked faithfully in her service for years leave without helping them make a new start. A former Capuchin writes, "The Roman insult by which I was reduced to the lay state stipulated that my order, which I had served to the best of my abilities for eighteen years, was free of any financial responsibility toward me." [4] Another priest says: "I am sixty years old. If I should lose the faith now and be obliged to leave the Church, I would have nothing, neither a place to retire nor social security. I couldn't even go to the Little Sisters of the Poor because they would reject me as a rene-

---

[4] In a letter to the monthly journal, *Lecture pour tous,* in response to an article entitled "Prêtres égarés," February–April, 1967.

gade." The same priest quoted the case of a nun who, after twenty-three years in her order, was "dismissed" because she returned to her religious house late after a visit to her family. She found herself in a garrett in Paris without a profession. One year later she became the mistress of a man who provided her with an apartment and clothing. (The situation of former nuns deserves another book.)

But cases like these are less frequent now, at least in some countries. In France the bishops have named a priest as head of the Society for Sacerdotal Assistance, an organization to assist those who leave. It is based on the idea—which is true —that those who leave are still brothers, that the Church to whose service they devoted the best years of their lives owes them this assistance. Laymen share in the activities of the Society for Sacerdotal Assistance. Former priests are lodged, given money for professional training and loans to support them while they are waiting to get established.

A good many priests who leave, however, are reluctant to call upon the services of this organization. They look upon it as a *charitable* institution and feel that they have a *right* to reimbursement proportionate to their years of dedication to the Church.

Very different is the work of the Servants of the Paraclete, founded in 1947 by Father Gerald Fitzgerald. The Paracletes are engaged in rehabilitating former priests. Two-thirds of the 1,600 priests they have worked with have returned to the ministry. They are presently establishing foundations in Europe. One of them, interestingly enough, is in Rome.

On the whole, and despite appreciable progress in recent years, the attitude of the Church toward priests who leave is not yet, in its material aspect, one of justice. This can be explained in part by the fear of encouraging defections. In

Sacerdotalis Caelibatus, Paul VI explained that the Church's discipline is "at once severe and merciful. It is without doubt a discipline that will confirm good priests in their determination to live lives of purity and holiness" and will at the same time "be a warning to those aspiring to the priesthood" (No. 89). The fear of destitution prevents many priests from leaving. But should they be kept at such a price? One can argue that a priest of fifty or sixty years of age who no longer believes in his priesthood but continues to exercise the ministry because it is too late for him to begin a new life is a realist. And we might add that realism is a Christian virtue. But it does nothing for priests who are resigned and without hope.

3. *A Special Case: The Delinquent Priest*

If a priest commits a crime simultaneous with or prior to his departure, the hierarchical authority often connives with the civil authorities to keep the affair quiet and avoid bringing him to trial. Civil authority at all levels—including the police chief who gives the delinquent priest ample warning of an impending arrest if he stays in the community—is happy to cooperate in this camouflage because the image of the priest, representing a certain popular morality, must not be altered in any way. As one psychiatrist has observed: "By refusing to admit that they are criminals, they become perverts. For they generally perservere in their crime and have the feeling that they are marginal men, different from others. When a priest or a former priest submits to trial in a court of law, we can cure him much more easily."

The Church, which is a sinful as well as a holy body, often consents to hypocrisy as the price of unavoidable human failures. To accept herself as an imperfect human society would no doubt be a better way to practice the true spirit of poverty.

4. What Authorities Say About Priests Who Leave

The last pontifical document that dealt with this question at any length was *Sacerdotalis Caelibatus*. The terms used to designate former priests are often crude and embarrassing. The pope says that "departed" priests remain "his dearly beloved brothers." But in speaking of them he is saddened by their "unhappy lot," their "unfortunate and lamentable state." He regrets their "misfortune" and says that it is always with "heartfelt regret" that the Church grants dispensations. He notes the "sorrow, dishonor and unrest" they cause the Church and refers to them as "deserters." No doubt some of this unfortunate terminology is the fault of translations. *Desertio*, for example, means "to leave." But its overtones are very negative. There is no suggestion that these departures might be explained by structural weaknesses in the Church. The only error Paul VI admits is that ecclesiastical authorities have not always discerned the qualities of candidates for the priesthood early enough.

It is always a question of "a fall" or "weakness" when priests leave. They are indiscriminately judged guilty. Some of them may be guilty. But others are men of exceptional quality and moral worth who made a mistake in choosing the priesthood and later corrected it. To admit this is not to diminish the merits of those who stay. And it is, furthermore, difficult to understand how it is possible to speak of "weakness" with reference to those who so courageously criticize the Church and the situation of the clergy.

Present attitudes, however, represent considerable progress. Formerly, priests who left were considered anathema. Seminarians were presented with horrifying images of "fallen" priests who were harshly forbidden all means of reconciliation unless, of course, they were important figures in the world. Talleyrand, who was a scoundrel of the first order, died fortified by the sacraments of the Church. But not Felicité de Lamennais who was buried clandestinely and civilly in a common plot on Ash Wednesday, 1854.

5. *Reactions of the Faithful—The Word "Defrocked"*

In his encyclical Paul VI speaks of "the scandal of the faithful." The word is not too strong. Priests who leave are still poorly received by the faithful and stir up severe judgments that sometimes extend to the clergy as a whole.

Some characteristic examples:

A priest was named to a country parish where the two previous pastors had left to marry. The first Catholic who came to visit him said: "Father, if you want to have some fun, ask us for the money to go to Paris. But don't carry on here. It does too much harm." Some time later another parishioner said, with more than a trace of irony in his voice: "You're a strong one. They haven't trapped you yet."

A young assistant lived with a pastor who had been his spiritual father and arranged to have him posted with him after ordination. The pastor was not only a father but a "mother hen" as well. In the end the assistant married a girl from the parish, as much to escape his pastor as to leave the ministry. The pastor tried at first to hide the truth from his parishioners. He hinted that his assistant was sick and had gone to a sanatorium in the mountains. But, as is usual in such cases, the truth soon became known. The pastor's philosophy was that laymen shouldn't invite young priests into their homes too often because if they came into contact with happy families they would be tempted to marry.

Some of the parishioners refused to discuss this affair. Others felt responsible for their former assistant. "We must stop him from doing this thing." "We must save him." Many condemned him. "He is damned." "It's diabolical." "This is a feminine trick." Some sought an explanation in his previous experience. "He went to too many meetings." "He never said all of his breviary." One father expressed fear for his seminarian son whose defiant attitude toward his superiors frightened him. "The way priests act today . . . I don't know where its all going to end." Only a few, it seemed, gave any thought to the lot of the priest in the Church and the world today or their own responsibilities in the matter.

These purely negative reactions can be explained by the very special bond that exists between the community and the priest. The community feels a kind of "jealous love" for him. They endow him with every virtue because they see themselves reflected in him. "It makes them feel good to love and be loved by so remarkable a man." [5] When he leaves, the community feels unworthy and inclined to reject him. Moreover, without wanting to admit as much, it also has a guilty conscience. The priest who leaves is in their eyes "defrocked." The dictionary points out that this word is always used ironically and contemptuously. That is why every effort must be made to banish it and why this book does not use it. But the fact remains that the negative reactions to a priest's defection, among practicing Catholics and even on the part of public opinion that is otherwise indifferent to the affairs of the Church, are very revealing.

In Catholic circles, where divorce is becoming more accepted, the "defrocked" priest is still a cause of embarrassment. The priest is usually considered a sacred person,[6] standing in special relationship to God. Anyone who breaks off such a relationship is automatically more guilty than anyone else. For a long time the priest was presented as a "man of God," placed on a pedestal and dehumanized. Non-Catholics themselves often contributed to his false image.

[5] Dr. J. Chavreul, "Affectivité du prêtre," *Christus*, No. 48, October, 1965.
[6] In the false sense of the term, which is to say as a man who has received with consecration quasi-magical privileges, rights and honors.

Moreover, by leaving the clerical society the priest upsets the established order, an order in which he was charged to represent a certain traditional morality. He is thus one who refuses to play his social role. And it is not always clear what other role he might play. If he finds one that suits him and succeeds in it, he is much better accepted.

The following factors must also be taken into consideration:

1. The ironical situation of a man who thought he was capable of living an uncommon life and failed.

2. Suspicion. The former priest is often considered a victim of obsession, homosexuality or mental illness. Some "shady background" is suspected.

3. Revenge. The former priest who once forgave sins and dispensed wise counsel is now seen as a sinner himself and a public one at that.

Again, we must bear in mind the progress that has been made in recent years. It is by no means exceptional for Catholics to maintain friendly relations with former priests. This is particularly true of intellectuals and workers. It also characterizes the clergy itself. The word "defrocked" is being replaced by such expressions as "a priest who has changed his way of life" and other paraphrases. Censorious attitudes are more rarely encountered. The fact that the attitude of the clergy in this matter is evolving more rapidly than that of the laity is also significant.

It is desirable, of course, that such progress continue. As the American psychologist E. Mark Stern writes: "In any case, I think we should have the compassion and intelligence to accept that a man or woman may leave the priesthood or convent for high moral, frequently inspired reasons, after great prayer and soul searching. Some leave because of problems which they couldn't cope with in the context of their vocation. That doesn't mean they were not honest when they entered the priesthood or convent. If we admit that man is an imperfect creature who looks for self-fulfillment, we must realize that he will change." [7]

AFTER DEPARTURE

It was long the custom in the Church to present the lot of priests who left as catastrophic. That tradition has not entirely disappeared. We have referred to Paul VI's condemnatory language. An article, drawing no doubt upon sources unknown to mere mortals, explains that "the priest who is unfaithful to his vows is overwhelmed with remorse and feels a veritable nostalgia for the priestly life." [8]

But what are the facts? Several elements must enter into any adequate answer to this question.

1. *Those Who Become Protestant Ministers or Orthodox Priests*

Their number, while not negligible, is comparatively small (at least in countries where the majority of the population is Catholic). But it is worth pointing out that more priests become Protestant ministers than vice versa.

Protestant churches for the most part are rather strict in selecting candidates for the ministry and have been far-sighted in providing structures of rehabilitation. The defection rate among ministers is also increasing although the Protestant community is as discreet on this subject as the Catholic Church, "so as not to interfere with good ecumenical relations," they explain.

It seems that priests who become ministers are generally successful. Their work remains fundamentally the same and often their style of life changes little. Considered as the out-

---

[7] E. Mark Stern, *Jubilee, op. cit.*, p. 19.
[8] Jean Egen, "Prêtres égarés," *Lectures pour tous*, February, 1967.

come of an intellectual and spiritual evolution, these cases do not provoke the negative reactions that reduction to the lay state does. They represent special cases which are important but by no means typical.

2. *Without Regrets?*

Here we must be careful to respect the individual flavor of each case. We may, however, make these general observations. Priests who leave are very sensitive to what others think of them and tend to be secretive about their former way of life. Some of them are neurotically sensitive. Realizing well along in life that they had made a mistake and having no one to blame, they cannot tolerate either criticism or assistance. None of them can bear pity. Very seldom do they admit that their departure may have been an error and their present life a failure. There is a tendency for former priests to be self-righteous, a state of mind that is often accompanied by guilt feelings.

Those who leave after an intellectual or spiritual evolution or a loss of faith rarely show signs of guilt. This is significant because social pressures normally would bring this out if it existed. "I realized," said a laicized priest, "that the priesthood was not my true vocation. After having given it serious thought, I sought another place in the Church as a layman. I have no regrets. I am at peace with myself and with the Church." Such former priests become outstanding laymen. "If I had it to do over again," says another, "I wouldn't hesitate a minute. I do not try to forget because I have nothing to forget. My way is not everyone's. But I have no regrets."

But others suffer from guilt, especially those who leave because of an affair, a bad stroke of luck, or because they felt incapable of realizing their ideal of what a priest should be. Some of them return to the priesthood. Others cannot, even if they wanted to, because they are married or for some other reason.

Those who did not have a true vocation and realized it too late as a rule do not regret their decision to leave (even though they may miss the prestige the ministry conferred upon them). The mentally ill are a special case. Some of them (especially those who are seriously sick) punish themselves by becoming beggars (one such case was discussed in Chapter II) or engaging in other forms of anti-social behavior.

3. Married Priests—Family Problems

A considerable segment of the Catholic population would like to see the marriages of priests fail. "The qualities that make a good priest make a good husband," they reason. "A bad priest will be a bad husband." Such hasty generalizations are often motivated by spite and contradicted by the fact of many happy marriages among former priests. Nonetheless there are real difficulties facing the priest who marries late in life, after he has already acquired the habits of a bachelor. The cloister is a poor preparation for marriage. His choice of a wife is not always a wise one. And those who marry to solve their sexual problems, looking upon woman as a "therapeutic," rarely make good husbands.

In almost all cases the former priest and his wife must meet their respective families. Generally, the priest's family (especially the mother) takes his departure badly, considering it a sin or a social disgrace. Even if she understands, she suffers from the spiteful attitudes and questions of friends or relatives. Thus the social status of the family is affected. Families that live in a ghetto or a closely knit community sometimes choose to move away and seek anonymity. In addition to the difficulties the former priest encounters with his own family, there are usually further problems with his wife's family. The fact of the matter is, the majority of Catholics are poorly prepared to accept the marriage of priests graciously or even with charity. There is, finally, the element of adverse material circumstances, which does not facilitate happy home life.

4. *Material Difficulties*

All priests who leave have the problem of finding suitable employment. In countries with a strong Catholic tradition, a clerical background is not the best possible reference. Quite the contrary, it would be better not to mention this fact. But then the problem arises of how to account for so many years of one's life. The former priest is then forced to lie in order to hide his past. The usual dissimulation is to say that he worked in the family business and had a fight with his father. But such fabrications rarely fool prospective employers.

This predicament is further aggravated because most priests are not professionally qualified. The obvious exception here is the priest who was a teacher. He readjusts easily enough in a secular environment. Some former priests choose to do manual labor and often become skilled workmen. Most, however, go into administration work, the social services, cultural organizations and research (in France, the National Center for Scientific Research numbers many former priests, some of them very well known, on its staff). Those who are still young enough often return to the university.

In the United States, William Restivo, a thirty-six-year-old former missionary in Kenya, founded a placement agency for former priests with offices in New York and five other major cities. His work is financed by Catholic laymen. Organizations of this kind are springing up in every country— sometimes spontaneously, sometimes under the direction of the local hierarchy.

There is also the problem of where to live. It is difficult for a former priest to stay where he exercised his ministry or to return to his home town. He must get away. He usually goes to a large city where anonymity is guaranteed. Sometimes he goes abroad. (In France, for example, many find employment in the new African states.)

To go against the whole world—parents, friends, Church and society—and admit that one has made a mistake, to confront, at an age when others have already arrived, the difficulties of new beginnings takes great courage. Some remain priests because they do not have such courage. Others remain for respectable reasons. "I couldn't do this to my parents," said one unhappy but resigned priest. Others remain because they are too old to start afresh. Most priests, we may be sure, remain because they believe in their ministry and feel no reason to question their commitment. They, too, need courage to bear up under the frustrations of their way of life. We are not interested here in anything so absurd as measuring the merits of those who remain against those who leave. We merely wish to point out that many more priests would leave if they were not restrained by the kind of circumstances we have pointed out.

Thus the number of those who do leave is not in itself an adequate indication of the crisis of the clergy. But it does give us some idea. And the reasons why they leave, which we have briefly analyzed, tell us something about the causes of the crisis.

PART TWO

Proposals for Those Who Remain and for Those to Come: Declericalization

1

The End of the Clergy

PRIESTS ARE NECESSARY to a Church. Without them, there could be no Church. The truth of this proposition is evident on a sociological basis. To exist, every institution needs the services of a few particularly devoted persons to promote its interests, whether on a permanent basis or not. Every ideology needs an institution if it is to influence men in a lasting fashion and not, duly labeled, be relegated to the dusty "classics" on a library shelf. This is equally true for the Church and Christianity.

But Christianity is much more than an ideology and the Church is more than an institution: it is the people of God, the sign of Christ, "the temporal and spatial extension of the Incarnation." [1] Thus priests are necessary on theological grounds. Long accused of being too content with a poor theology of the priesthood, specialists are now attacking the problem. They teach that all Christians are responsible for all the Church but that the priest is "responsible for the responsible." [2] The Council specified that the priest shares in the ministry of Christ by building up His Body which is the Church. In other words, the link between the Church and Christ is realized in the priest. He is not for that reason a superman but rather a man in the service of others. The Council document on the Church recalls that Christians do

[1] F. Varillon, "Un abrégé de la foi Catholique," *Etudes,* October, 1967.
[2] Henri Denis, *Prêtre de demain* (Paris, Casterman).

not exist for the ministers but the ministers for Christians. A priest is no more another Christ than any Christian. But he should be just as much so. The expression *sacerdos alter Christus* is applicable to all Christians who share in the royal priesthood of "the people of God" and who must all strive to be other Christs with full knowledge that they will never be able to perfectly achieve this idea.

This link between Christ and the Church is particularly marked in the Eucharist which is accomplished by the Church. "The priest is indispensable. But when he offers the sign of the Body and Blood of Christ, it is clear that he no longer has any power over this sign. He must surrender to it like any other Christian." [3]

Some theologians are inclined to emphasize preaching the Word of God as the essential function of the Church. The priest must participate in this mission like other Christians and even lead others, if it is to be the work of the Church. But the Word is intrinsically bound up with the Eucharist. Preaching unites us to Christ in the Eucharist. Therefore the priest is also indispensable in this capacity. "A Church of laymen could spread Christianity in the world but it would be at most a Christianity without Christ, a mere ideology." [4]

There seems to be wide agreement among theologians on these definitions. They correspond to the experience of the nontheological laymen who feel the need of the Eucharist to approach God and of the priest to celebrate the Eucharist, to set the example of an evangelical life and preach the Word. They also correspond to the experience of the Church and the demands of the specialized world of today. Experts in theology and the pastorate are necessary to help man resolve his religious problems and aid the community to exist and develop.

[3] Henri Denis, "Le Prêtre dans le monde," in *Prêtres comment?* (Paris, Editions Ouvrières).
[4] *Ibid.*

It is clear that the Church needs priests and that the priest is specified by his mission. But it is not so clear that he need be specified by a certain style of life (as is, in principle at least, the religious). History teaches us that the status of the priest changes with circumstances. "To signify its spiritual message, the Church has forbidden the clergy to exercise certain professions, required a special form of clothing and recommended extreme political caution in some countries. At other times she has recommended that they work manually (especially on the missions), forbidden then to wear distinctive clothing and encouraged them to translate charity into 'temporal' service to 'others or to the common good.'"[5] The Church recognizes that the priest is not specified by his way of life and permits great diversity in this matter. Among the worker-priest, the country pastor, the curial bureaucrat, the priest-scientist, the writer, the professor and the editor there are great differences. They are accepted and sometimes desired by the Church.

However, in practice the same style of life is imposed on almost all priests in what regards work. Let us go further: in the West the same way of life is imposed on all priests in what regards celibacy. In other words, the priest theoretically is not specified by his way of life but in practice he is. And when he shows a desire to change this way of life, it is as though the pillars of the temple were collapsing.

Here again, history furnishes an explanation. It shows how priests were constituted as a social body called the clergy, with its proper hierarchy, its jurisdictions, its customs, and so forth. In the beginning, the Christian priesthood followed the example of Christ who had opposed the Levitic society, the priestly caste. But very rapidly the Church betrayed her origins. She secreted a new class, a force of considerable

[5] R. Salaün and E. Marcus, *Qu'est-ce qu'un prêtre?* (Paris, Editions du Seuil).

social importance: the clergy. But we must not be too quick to cast stones. After the fall of the Roman Empire, the western Church was the only stable institution in a disorganized world. It was inevitable that she strengthen her position, organize a hierarchy of functions, and even assume temporal power. Later, in the Middle Ages, to reject the feudal system would very likely have meant banishment from society for the priest. Incarnation for the Church probably required her to conform to the feudal mold. Those who are critical of the medieval Church today are strongly inconsistent with themselves. For they are precisely the ones who call for the Church to adapt to modern society and preach the desirability of pluralism, even within the Church. A respect for pluralism is also an attitude that can be explained historically. The constitution of the clergy as a separate caste could perhaps have been justified in the Middle Ages. But this does not mean that it can be justified today. One of the astonishing anomalies of history is how this clerical society has survived so long and shown vitality enough to seize the Church to its own profit.

The role of the Council of Trent in this matter was determining. It codified the situation inherited from the past, thus freezing it for the indefinite future at a time when it should have been adapting to the new evolution of the world and man. Trent's work in this matter was facilitated by the conviction that a clerical society was more necessary than ever in those countries where Catholicism had become the minority religion. These uneasy, closed communities could only find identity by gathering around a stable social body. Thus we should not perhaps judge the Council Fathers of Trent too harshly. Their successors, so reluctant to question the Tridentine achievement, are much more to blame. Too, that the clerical society gathered at Vatican II could admit it had seized the Church is to its credit and must be interpreted as a mark of docility to the Holy Spirit. But Vatican II, it would seem, did not go far enough. In particular, it did not see that the clergy must be done away with. It still hesitates to destroy itself. The instinct of conservation operates in societies as well as in individuals.

The seizure of the Church by the clerical society needs no lengthy demonstration. The invitation to a few laymen, chosen arbitrarily and in most cases already functionaries in the Church, to attend the Council was looked upon as something altogether exceptional. The same is true of the 1967 Synod. The Spirit breathes where it will. As it happened, the laymen, at the Synod especially, had something to say that did not quite correspond to what was expected of them. They were immediately accused of immaturity. That is possible. But whose fault is it?

Nor does the continuing presence of the clerical society need lengthy demonstration. When a priest works outside of the system, the Church is hard put to acommodate him. This is notably the case of priests engaged in scientific research. At a press conference in Rome (October, 1967), Bishop Marty, vice-president to the permanent council of the French episcopacy, said that such clerics, and there is a relatively large number of them, are completely on their own and that many of them leave. "We have not yet found a way," he said, "of sustaining them in their vocation. That is my nightmare."

This was also the problem with the first experiments with the worker-priests. The clerical society won the battle and succeeded in imposing its will: either the worker-priests had to be regularized or give up their priesthood. But a new worker-priest movement has been authorized, and those engaged in it today find it extremely difficult to maintain liaison with the clerical society, as they were asked to do. This problem is almost insoluble in the present state of things. Priests are expected to be both in the clergy and out of it.

That they are expected to show their deep and real solidarity with the Church is an altogether different matter. The Church is not and should not be the clerical society.

There are two related problems here. The Church must be given back to all the people of God, priests included. No one owns the Church. Secondly, the clerical society must be destroyed. And this for three reasons:

1. It is oppressive for its members and is a large factor in the present crisis of the priesthood. The preceding chapters of this book were intended to show this.

Some pretend, and many believe, that no matter how intolerable is the priest's condition, God's grace is there to help him. Happily! But grace builds on nature. Why do we persist in creating difficult problems for the priest when there is no evident need to? To be sure, every Christian life is marked with the sign of the cross. But Christ did not ask even his apostles to impose unnecessary burdens upon themselves. There may be some merit in doing so, provided one is properly motivated and avoids masochistic deviations. This in principle is why religious orders were founded. But the secular priest is not a religious; he chooses to perform a certain function in the Church. Moreover, we are not arguing that his life should be one of ease. It will always be difficult to be a priest in the modern world.

2. The existence of a clergy gives rise to serious doubts about the future of the ministerial priesthood. We must ask ourselves if men-priests will be necessary to the Church in the future. Many young men would gladly become priests if they were not obliged to become members of the clergy. And many priests would remain so if the style of clerical life had not become intolerable for them.

Thomas Aquinas held that God would never abandon his Church to the point where there were not enough qualified ministers to provide for the needs of the faithful. But

Thomas Aquinas was not divinely inspired. Are there enough qualified ministers in Brazil? We cannot blame God for our own mistakes.

There is deep concern over the lack of priests on a continent like Latin America. Missionaries cannot fill the gap. Moreover, they can never learn the mentality of the people they serve. The population of South America will be 300 million in 1980 and 600 million in the year 2000. How could one ever hope to recruit enough native priests when an important percentage (23–70 percent, depending on the country) of the population is illiterate and when, moreover, men who might otherwise be disposed to become priests would have to enter the clerical society?

3. The existence of a clergy with a special style of life is harmful to the missionary activity of the Church. This flows logically from the Council of Trent which conceived the Church as a fortress, with an organized clergy whose primary purpose was the conservation of the faith, not the conversion of souls. This is so evident that when it was decided to send priests into the world of the workers they were advised to adapt to the condition of the working man and thus abandon the clerical condition.[6] If the authority that authorized this experiment was wrong, why was it renewed? And if right, why don't we draw all the consequences from it, especially at a time when the whole Church, including the clergy, is urged to be missionary? It is said that the missionary "must be present to the world." Isn't this an admission that he is absent? Can this expression be applied to the layman? No, because he is already in the world, for better or worse. Only priests imprisoned in a clerical ghetto, or what comes to the same thing, clerical laymen, could invent the duty "to be present to the world."

[6] This is almost impossible to do successfully. The priest cannot know the worker's insecurity and, not being married, cannot experience the same difficulties and joys of life.

If the priest is separated by his style of life from the community of men, he cannot fulfill his missionary role as a priest. "Priests . . . live on earth with other men as brothers. The Lord Jesus, the Son of God, a Man sent by the Father to men, dwelt among us and willed to become like His brethren in all things except sin. . . . Priests by their vocation and ordination, are in a certain sense set apart in the bosom of the people of God. However, they are not to be separated from the people of God or from any person; but they are to be totally dedicated to the work for which the Lord has chosen them." [7] The limited character of the separation is clear.

In conclusion, the interests of the Church and her mission as well as the interests of all (priests and laity) who serve this mission would seem to combine to necessitate the dissolution of the clergy. Only on this condition can laymen feel responsible for the Church. They are constantly told that they are responsible. But how can they be? Where can they find their place in a society of clerics without abandoning their lay condition? Some laymen seem to be totally clericalized without favor of the sacrament of orders.

Of course, most laymen ask for nothing. They are too paralyzed by bad habits to be interested in taking on responsibilities. Only a few are willing to volunteer their services. Most are not displeased that the clerical society has seized the Church. This permits them to let others do the work, to criticize and yet avail themselves of the services the Church offers. They cling to the old image of the priest, even though they wouldn't want it for their sons. They are the ones who protest most loudly when changes come, as indeed they must.

We have no choice. Let them complain and let us try to convince them. But let us not desist. Is the Church what she says she is—the people of God—or not? That is the question

[7] *Decree on the Ministry and Life of Priests,* No. 3.

that must be answered. And the price that must be paid is the dissolution of the clergy, "the declericalization of the priest," to use Father Oraison's expression. How can the priest be declericalized? The following chapters will address themselves to this question.

2

Married Priests

CELIBACY IS STILL a taboo subject. In most countries priests have to discuss it in quasi-secrecy. They fear calumny and suspicion. Experience proves that their fears are not without foundation. Moreover, studies on celibacy which disapprove of the present rules are bound to stir up a tempest of insults against the author. If he is a journalist or a writer, he is accused of being "sensational" of seeking profit. It is sometimes suggested that the press has created the problem.

The impression is often given that celibacy is the most important of Christ's laws. In point of fact, it is not Christ's law at all. So there is no point in pretending that approval of the present system is a decisive mark of Christian authenticity, superior even to the beatitudes and the commandment of love. The Jesuit Father Heckel furnishes an example of this distorted emphasis: "The reality of consecrated chastity operates in the Church and in the world like a revelation, laying bare the profound meaning each of us gives to human existence. Each time that we, priests and laymen, fail to understand this, *it is a sign that the spirit of the Gospel is atrophying in us*" (italics added).[1]

[1] Commentary on the encyclical *Sacerdotalis Caelibatus*, *Cahiers d'action religieuse et sociale*, July, 1967.

The lack of serenity in this controversy is in itself an argument against celibacy. Both sides are guilty of excesses. Some priests call for the abrogation of the law with brutal and naïve passion.

It takes a good deal of courage to dare question a law which the supreme authority of the pope has just reaffirmed in an encyclical letter. But this encyclical didn't close all the doors. It is strongly in favor of maintaining the law of celibacy but it does not preclude some other solution in the future. From the point of view of research, an encyclical is more a step along the way than a final word. If this were not the case, the Church's thinking would be paralyzed. Moreover, this encyclical does not involve papal infallibility, a dogma that is singularly restrictive. The pope can always be wrong, even in encyclicals, except in those rare instances when he defines a dogmatic or moral truth *ex cathedra*. On the other hand, a pontifical text of this magnitude, published after long reflection, obviously merits our closest attention. "We have," wrote the pope, "for sometime earnestly implored the enlightenment and assistance of the Holy Spirit, and have examined before God opinions and petitions that have come to us from all over the world, notably from some pastors of God's Church" (No. 2). The pope, moreover, enumerates at length the objections against celibacy—which shows that he is aware of them—before giving the reasons which in his mind make it binding.

Our references to the encyclical itself will, therefore, be frequent.

Let us begin with a distinction. Chastity and celibacy are not the same thing. Chastity is a virtue—"a revolutionary virtue," said Lenin—which all Christians are obliged to practice, whether married or not. Celibacy is a state of life.

Must this state of life be imposed on all priests? That is the question.

The New Testament sheds little light on the problem. "The New Testament, which preserves the teaching of Christ and the apostles, does not demand celibacy of sacred ministers, but proposes it rather as a free act of obedience to a special vocation or a special spiritual gift (cf. Matt. 19:11-12). Jesus Himself did not make it a requisite in His choice of the Twelve, nor did the apostles for those who presided over the first Christian communities (cf. I Tim. 3:2-5; Tit. 1:5-6)" (No. 5).

On the contrary, Christ insisted primarily on the perfect spirit of poverty. This, if anything, is the *sine qua non* condition imposed on those who would follow Him. The parable concerning the rich young man is very clear in this regard. Hans Küng argues that the law of celibacy can scarcely be justified by the New Testament, in which total freedom for all Christians with respect to marriage and continence is safeguarded. Other theologians quote St. Paul who was especially prolix on this subject. For example: "He that is without a wife is solicitous for the things that belong to the Lord, how he may please God. But he that is with a wife is solicitous for the things of the world, how he may please his wife. And he is divided" (I Corinthians 7:32-33). Or: "But I say to the unmarried and to the widows: it is good for them to so continue, even as I. But if they do not contain themselves, let them marry. For it is better to marry than to be burnt" (I Corinthians 7:8-9). Again: "But I speak this by indulgence, not by commandment" (I Corinthians 7:6). These pragmatic counsels seem somewhat contradictory, and it is not evident from the context that they are intended primarily for priests.

Thus the New Testament furnishes no clear recommendations. If it did, the Church would always have had a clear-cut stand toward clerical celibacy. But celibacy was not

required of priests in the early ages of the western Church
and still isn't everywhere.

History tells us it was the Council of Elvira in the fourth
century that first made celibacy obligatory for clerics, but it
was not until the twelfth century that it was firmly established and only with the Council of Trent was it solemnly
ratified. We also learn from history that not all the reasons
for this legislation were good ones. The fact that children of
married clerics could inherit ecclesiastical property was
scarcely pleasing to medieval popes and emperors. There was
great ignorance about sex, as there was even a century ago,
and the dominant spirit seems to have been best summarized
by St. Jerome (in a formula that still inspires many churchmen today): *Omnis coitus immundus*—all sexual intercourse
is impure. For this reason, sexual intercourse and the celebra-
tion of the Eucharist were considered incompatible.

In his book *Marriage and Celibacy*, Max Thurian explains
this contempt for sex in terms of the depraved morals of the
decadent Greco-Roman civilization. "Confronted with widespread immorality, Christians desired to imitate the purity
of Christ and practice true love. They consequently exaggerated the ideals of virginity and continence. The many per-
versions of sexuality were a cause of disgust and marriage
itself came to be frowned upon. There is nothing surprising
in the fact that voluntary celibacy came to be considered
morally superior to marriage."

But we are not trying to find a decisive argument in history. It is not because the practice of celibacy is relatively
recent that it must be considered as an altogether transitory
phenomenon destined to disappear. Nor is it because inadequate reasons have been mingled with more weighty ones in
an attempt to justify the present ruling that it must be condemned. Neither is it, inversely, because the practice has

been observed for centuries that it must be continued. Paul VI, however, uses this argument: "It is unthinkable that for centuries the Church of the West has followed a path that, instead of favoring the spiritual richness of individual souls and of the people of God, has in some way compromised it, or that she has with arbitrary juridical prescriptions stifled the free expansion of the most profound realities of nature and of grace" (No. 41). No doubt. But circumstances change and new rules may be more appropriate. Humanity should not seek laws for today in its history; otherwise it would be imprisoned in and paralyzed by its past, although this is not to deny that history furnishes guidelines for present-day action.

Clerical celibacy is not universally required. Since the time of Pius XII the western Church has admitted married men to orders. Not a great many, to be sure, but the exceptions prove that the rule is not irrevocable. And in the eastern Churches there is a large body of married clergy. About one-third of the Maronite clergy is married. In Iraq, 17 of the 152 Chaldean and Syrian Catholic priests are married. The only statistics we have for the Greek Catholics are from the patriarchate of Damascus (which may be taken as indicative): eight out of 27 priests are married.[2] The eastern Churches admit married men to the priesthood as a matter of course, although they cannot marry after they are ordained or remarry if their wife dies. Nor can married priests become bishops. On the whole the celibate clergy is elderly, and since the nineteenth century has decreased in numbers. Some eastern bishops favor celibacy. But the Maronite patriarch Paul-Pierre Meouchi, a cardinal of the Catholic Church, raises this question: "Should we leave entire regions without priests because we do not want a married clergy which has in

[2] Statistics quoted by Robert Clément, S.J., "La vie du clergé marié en Orient," in *Proche-Orient Chrétien*, 1966.

the past and continues to render admirable services for the salvation of souls? Should we let these regions be deprived of the spiritual food of the Word of God and the sacraments of the Church because we are reluctant to permit a married clergy?" [3]

Cardinal Bea said at the Council that married priests in the eastern Church "do not represent a concession." And Bishop Edelby, auxiliary to Maximos IV, pointed out in a lecture in Rome that "a vocation to the diaconate or priesthood is different from a vocation to celibacy which requires a special grace."

The Council also recognized the legitimacy of the eastern tradition. In the *Decree on the Ministry and Life of Priests* (No. 16), it spoke of "married priests of the highest merit" and exhorted them "to persevere in their holy vocation so that they may fully and generously continue to expend themselves for the sake of the flock commended to them." In his encyclical Paul VI lauded the eastern married clergy in similar terms. With the Council Fathers he admitted that virginity "is not demanded by the very nature of the priesthood as is apparent from the practice of the early Church." Rather "celibacy has a many-faceted suitability for the priesthood."

Thus there is no necessary connection between celibacy and the priesthood, on either historical or geographical grounds. Celibacy cannot be supported by intrinsic arguments, only by "arguments of convenience." We must now judge their value.

The first kind of argument advanced by the partisans of obligatory celibacy is utilitarian. The married priest, they say, cannot be "all to all." A prisoner of human love, he cannot totally love all men. Concern for his family will interfere with his work as a priest. This argument is usually advanced by

[3] In a letter dated February 27, 1964. Quoted by Robert Clément, *op. cit.*

those Catholics who are poorly informed on the question
(which is to say the great majority of them). We might
answer that married men—doctors, professors, and so forth
—have in fact shown great accessibility to all men. Marriage
may even favor this disposition. The Protestant churches
whose ministers are married, have had their martyrs. The
wives of German ministers encouraged their husbands to
profess their faith against Nazi paganism. "The married
priests of the Eastern Churches, "Bishop Edelby pointed out,
"helped save the faith in times of persecution because of
their family and professional roots in our villages." The
family can be a deep source of strength. The married clergy
of the East who were interviewed by Father Clément generally agreed on the following points:

"The missionary activity of my wife is unquestionably a
great help to me in my ministry."

"Marriage makes my home life more pleasant and frees me
for service to the parish."

"Despite material difficulties, my marriage does not interfere with my religious duties because my family and I have
a clear understanding of the priest's responsibilities. I chose
to become a priest to serve God and my family first of all."

"To have children brings one very close to life and gives
us a better understanding of the problems of others."

Of the ninety-seven priests interviewed by Father Clément, only five thought celibacy was more compatible with
the ministry.

The utilitarian argument in favor of celibacy can be counterbalanced by other utilitarian arguments against it (not including those mentioned in the first part of this book). For
example, there is no doubt that celibacy diminishes the number of vocations to the priesthood. Protestantism is also experiencing a vocation crisis, which proves that celibacy is
not the only obstacle. But almost every survey taken among

young people shows that it is nonetheless a very real one. Yet hundreds of millions of men throughout the world have the right to be evangelized.

Furthermore, family life contributes to psychic health. The absence of family responsibility retards maturity. Priests are so conscious of this frustration that they sometimes try to create artificial families. In France the rural clergy has undertaken a revealing experiment: "Just as old people are taken care of by their families, so, too, teams of priests could take care of their aged and sick. Seminarians might also become members of these teams." [4]

The utilitarian reasons for obligatory celibacy are not, therefore, convincing. Arguments and counterarguments could be drawn up indefinitely without coming to any decisive conclusion.

More impressive is the argument which holds that celibacy is a sign. As the Council said: "They give, moreover, a living sign of the world to come . . . in which the children of the resurrection neither marry nor take wives." [5] Paul VI also stresses this argument: "In the world of man, so deeply involved in earthly concerns and too often enslaved by the desires of the flesh (cf. I John 2:16), the precious divine gift of perfect continence for the kingdom of heaven stands out precisely as 'a singular sign of the blessings of heaven.' It proclaims the presence on earth of the final stages of salvation (cf. I Cor. 7:29-31) with the arrival of a new world; and in a way it anticipates the fulfillment of the kingdom as it sets forth its supreme values that will one day shine forth in all the children of God" (No. 34).

This is a worthy motive. But a sign must be efficacious. It must be perceived by and intelligible to men in a given age.

---

[4] Report on the social role of the priest, a seminar held at Issy-les-Moulineaux in 1965 and published in *Prêtres comment* (Paris, Editions ouvrières).
[5] *Decree on the Ministry and Life of Priests*, No. 16.

This does not seem to be the case today. Aspirants to the priesthood themselves do not seem convinced by this argument. Here is one item of evidence: "I have often asked seminarians. 'Why are priests required to take a vow of chastity?' What am I to think of answers to the effect that marriage and apostolic action are incompatible, that marriage does not give one enough freedom, that it endangers the seal of the confessional, and so forth? And what am I to think of those who say that celibacy is the only true way to show our love for Christ?" [6] For much greater reason, lay Catholics are generally incapable of articulating the meaning of celibacy. As for unbelievers, most of them don't think that the celibate is sincere. They suspect that he is carrying on clandestine affairs or practicing homosexuality.

The Church places great importance upon signs. But signs which have a value in one age do not automatically retain that value in another. If signs become imperceptible, are they still useful? And can someone be forced into a symbolic role against his aspirations and abilities? Celibacy would undoubtedly be more meaningful if aspirants to the priesthood were given a choice, if they accepted it gladly and were able to give clear reasons for their choice. This is not the case, however. It is often objected that celibacy is not an obligation but a "gift." Both the Council and the pope use the term. The encyclical says: "It is therefore the task of those who hold authority in the Church to determine, in accordance with the varying conditions of time and place, who in actual practice are to be considered suitable candidates for the religious and pastoral service of the Church, and what should be requested of them" (No. 15). It is clearly a disciplinary obligation. It does not become a gift until "those who participate in the priesthood of Christ through the

[6] F. Marchand, "Problèmes de chasteté et petit seminaire," in the supplement to *la Vie spirituelle*, February, 1967.

Sacrament of Orders humbly and fervently pray for it," [7] which is to say, if celibacy is chosen for itself. In principle this choice pertains to the vocation of religious, not all priests. Even when it is freely accepted, not all problems disappear but there is more clear-mindedness about them.

A third type of argument for celibacy is more elevated. It is, as the specialists say, "Christological." It holds that the priest must be totally dedicated to Christ, the eternal priest. Paul VI's encyclical draws upon this argument several times:

"This deep connection between celibacy and the priesthood of Christ is reflected in those whose fortune it is to share in the dignity and in the mission of the Mediator and Eternal Priest; this sharing will be more perfect the freer the sacred minister is from the bonds of flesh and blood" (No. 21).

"This, then, is the mystery of the newness of Christ, of all that He is and stands for; it is the sum of the highest ideals of the Gospel and of the kingdom; it is a particular manifestation of grace, which springs from the pascal mystery of the Savior and renders the choice of celibacy desirable and worthwhile on the part of those called by our Lord Jesus Christ. Thus, they intend not only to participate in Christ's priestly office, but also to share with Him His very condition of living" (No. 23).

These are magnificent texts. They convincingly demonstrate the close connection between the sacerdotal ministry and celibacy. Nevertheless, two qualifications are in order.

1. The priest is not Christ's successor, his lieutenant, his representative on earth. The whole Church is, the Body of Christ. This is the locus and instrument of Christ's action in the world. It would not do to elevate the priest above the Church. He is a servant of the Church which is the larger reality. The Church is the people of God, the royal priest-

[7] *Decree on the Ministry and Life of Priests*, No. 16.

hood. Since this is so, are not all members of the Church, lay-men as well as priests, called to imitate Christ in the same way? And if this is the case, why require celibacy of priests and not of the laity? Has it not been traditionally the religi-ous who seek higher states of perfection, more perfect con-formity with Christ? [8] The loftier the motives for celibacy, the more restricted its appeal. It seems imperative that we distinguish between the secular priest's state of life and that of the religious. In practice the differences between them are scarcely perceptible (unless the religious is a monk) and many priests complain of being "religious in spite of them-selves." Some even accuse the religious orders of "imperial-ism." It is worth noting that almost all of the books in favor of celibacy have been written by religious.

2. The impressive internal logic of *Sacerdotalis Caelibatus* does not hold up when we recall that there are as a matter of fact married priests and the encyclical lauds them on several occasions. Are they not also totally dedicated to Christ? Are they to be considered second-rate priests? This does not seem to be the mind of Paul VI, who expresses great esteem for them, or that of the Council, which renders homage to them. They are simply priests of a different way of life. The Catho-lic priesthood is not expressed, and never has been, in any one way.

In his encyclical Paul VI points out that the particular situation in the eastern clergy is due "to the different histori-cal background of that noble part of the Church, a situation that the Holy Spirit has providentially and supernaturally influenced" (No. 38). No one will deny that historical differ-ences are important factors. It is, therefore, a question of opportuneness. Might we not, then, judge it opportune to

---

[8] It is curious that a religious who becomes a secular priest is dispensed from his vows of poverty and obedience. Does this mean the secular priests do not imitate Christ in these respects?

have married priests in the western Church today since married men are ordained?

There are a number of objections against this. They are serious and must be examined carefully.

The first objection is that a married clergy is an inferior clergy. The example of the married eastern clergy, who are looked down upon as "peasants" by the educated faithful, might be adduced as evidence of this. It is true that this zealous and morally worthy clergy is too ignorant. But not because they are married. Eastern priests are for the most part recruited without concern for their education. The bishop and the parishioners themselves are interested in a man of goodwill who can carry out the charge of a pastorate. He rarely receives a suitable intellectual or spiritual formation. But if married priests were carefully recruited and properly trained, there is no reason why they should be second rate. There is a much greater danger that a married diaconate be second rate. Yet this institution is meeting with wide approval.

A second objection is that not all marriages are successes and the failure of a priest's marriage could be interpreted as a countersign. Not necessarily. Here is a psychiatrist's expert opinion: "A man who lacks sexual and emotional maturity (the two go together) and who cannot therefore achieve an integrated life is not made for either marriage or the priesthood. He must first find his balance and then make his decision. Marriage is not a therapeutic any more than is a religious vocation. However, many people think sexual difficulties not only indicate the lack of a religious vocation but point clearly to marriage. They think that marriage is an opportunity to satisfy one's instincts, that it opens the 'sluice gates' as it were and consequently promotes equilibrium. Nothing could be more false, for from a human point of view marriages can fail just as religious vocations can. The opposition that is commonly postulated between marriage and a religious vocation does not seem to me valid. Likewise, conjugal chastity and celibate chastity are often opposed. In light of Christian ideals, one is as difficult as the other. We may even ask whether the former is not more difficult." [9]

If marriage is looked upon as an easy solution, where anything goes, it will surely end in catastrophe. But only a celibate could think of it as an easy solution. It is a state of life that calls for different virtues, virtues than are sometimes very difficult to practice.

Precisely because marriage is not an easy solution, it can fail. There are flagrant failures of celibacy as well; yet this is no reason to condemn the celibate state as such. The hierarchical authority, moreover, could protect itself in two ways. First, sanctions like suspension could be applied to priests whose marriages were a cause of scandal. Secondly, the quality of the marriage of those being admitted to orders would be carefully investigated.

A third objection holds that married priests would have great difficulty supporting their families. This objection is not valid for all countries or in all cases. Some priests have the means to lead a comfortable life and raise a family. But the majority no doubt do not. Two things can be done for them. First of all, the Church should guarantee them a decent living. The present situation cannot be tolerated much longer even if priests don't marry. We shall have more to say about this later. Secondly, married priests could hold professional positions, in which case they would have no more difficulty raising a family than the average layman or deacon. In any case, the financial objection is a weak one.

A fourth objection goes like this: the fact that a man lives with a woman and has children by her does not mean that he will be closer to others. Married men can be just as selfish as

[9] Dr. Le Moal, "Formation de la chasteté," in *La Vocation, op. cit.*

celibates. This is true, with one important qualification. The objection, to be exact, should be corrected to read: "the *mere* fact." Marriage does not automatically endow one with the ability to understand others. Still, to share the same lot as the majority of men in a world where most people are married facilitates such understanding. There are many ways of sharing the common lot of mankind, of becoming a man among men, and marriage is one of them. But it is not a panacea for the crisis in the Catholic priesthood. Similar crises among the Orthodox and Protestants show clearly enough that celibacy is not the only or even the principal cause of the crisis. The first part of this book tried, among other things, to point this out. A married clergy cannot, therefore, be the only solution to the crisis. A total solution necessarily involves a revolution in our conception of how the ministerial priesthood should be exercised.

A married clergy would contribute to the declericalization of priests. Moreover, the witness of a married priest, supporting a family and confronting the same difficulties as other men and yet being all to all, would have great value as a sign. Celibacy, for those who chose it freely, would then recover its full symbolism. For to accept married priests would be in no way to deny the high value of celibacy. It is simply to recognize the diversity of vocations.

There is one final question. If we admit that the Church can ordain married men, can we also admit that priests who are now celibate could receive permission to marry? This is hard to answer, although it is being asked in many countries.

One strong objection immediately presents itself: if such permission were granted, it would unquestionably cause scandal among the laity. It would seem as though the priest were being released from his commitment while the layman remains bound by his. For most Catholics the indissolubility of marriage and the practice of celibacy are closely related

A Church Without Priests?

and raise the same kind of problem. If priests receive permission to marry, why shouldn't the Church be more lenient with respect to divorce and remarriage, especially since the present regulations cause such painful dramas? Such discrimination—liberality for some and severity for others—would be scandalous. The scandal, in fact, has already begun to the extent that priests are more readily reduced to the lay state than marriages were annulled.

Priests might answer that when they took their vows they were more conditioned than free and consequently did not give full consent when they committed themselves. But many laymen could say as much.

Another argument in favor of marriage for priests already ordained is much more solid. The indissolubility of marriage and fidelity to celibacy are not in fact the same kind of problem at all. Marriage is a sacrament, celibacy is not.[10] The indissolubility of marriage is of divine right while celibacy is a positive law of the Church. The latter is merely a disciplinary measure and not "by nature" intrinsic to the sacrament of orders. Since the Church imposed the rule, she can remove it without affecting the sacrament. This is not true of marriage. It is "by nature" indissoluble. This argument seems irrefutable. But we cannot expect it to be grasped by the generality of laymen who have a very meager theological education. Might they not interpret it as a subtle effort to justify a privilege for priests which is being denied them? Indeed they might!

It seems advisable, then, to outline a general strategy to solve this difficult question.

[10] Some theologians go further and make a distinction between the very nature of the sacrament of marriage and the sacrament of orders. They conclude that the latter should be exercised on a temporary basis only. It isn't likely that this theory will ever be accepted. But however impossible, it would constitute another argument for a married clergy.

1. It is mandatory to bring an end to the uncertainty that prevails now. As Father Oraison has stressed: "The confused and unformulated hope that they will one day be able to marry and remain priests . . . is of no help to the interested parties. It can only lead to malaise and further objections against celibacy." [11]

Paul VI's encyclical did not end the uncertainty. Many think that what the pope has done can be undone by another pope or Council. A solemn act of the Church united in Council or a Synod, after serious consultation with all priests and an in-depth sounding of lay opinion (a sounding only, for it is not the place of the laity to decide how priests should live their lives), is therefore necessary if this problem is to be resolved. Only through dialogue will priests today, impregnated as they are with the mentality of modern man, accept the final decision—especially if it means giving up all hope of marrying.

This might have the added advantage of clarifying regional differences throughout the world and thus furnishing a further guide to action. In some areas, priests already ordained could marry without major inconvenience; in others, they might be asked to make additional sacrifices as the last generation not to have an option. Such sacrifices would be justified by the common good of the Christian communities to which they dedicated their lives rather than by arbitrary authoritarianism; such sacrifices would have high symbolic value for which the laity would owe the priests a debt of gratitude. Almost all priests would understand this and, presumably, accept it. Moreover, the idea of progress has conditioned us not to expect the benefits the next generation will enjoy.

2. To avoid multiplying sacrifices of this kind, it would

[11] Marc Oraison, *le Célibat* (Paris, Editions du Centurion).

have to be made very clear that future priests could marry, that henceforward all aspirants to the priesthood would have an option between two states of life.

3. If this policy were established, it might be possible for some priests already ordained to benefit by it in exceptional cases. Dispensations from celibacy accompanied by a mandatory return to the lay state, no matter how readily granted, do not solve the problem of those who wish *to marry and still remain priests.*

At the same time it would no doubt be opportune and legitimate to show a more liberal attitude toward petitions for marriage annulments. For there is little doubt that some laymen had as little interior freedom when they married as some priests when they accepted celibacy.

4. It would seem eminently desirable that in light of recent discoveries in psychology, specialists study the validity of *lifelong commitments.* The lives of many men and women have in effect been ruined by the burden of obligations contracted without real freedom. This certainly could not have been Christ's will. In the Gospels, interestingly enough, Christ made many promises to his apostles but asked none of them. On the contrary, each time one of them committed himself spontaneously, Christ went out of his way to show him he could not remain faithful to it.

5. A considerable program of theological education for both priests and laymen ought to be initiated. The lack of such an education is a serious obstacle to progress at the present time. It is not merely a question of understanding and accepting the new image of the priest. What is necessary is to know what a priest is.

All of these proposals are arguable. Several of them seem to correspond to widespread opinion, considerable enough at least to be seriously discussed. Do they have any chance of success, things being what they are?

A joke that made the rounds at Vatican II had two bishops standing in St. Peter's Square. They were discussing a married clergy. "Do you think we will live to see that day?" one of them asked. The other answered: "We won't. But our children will." It does not seem desirable to wait another generation before giving candidates to the priesthood a choice between the two states of life.

Some think the innovation of a married diaconate will lead inevitably to a married priesthood. This is possible. Once married men are admitted as clerics, a breach will have been made. Most of the bishops who voted against a married diaconate at the Council were afraid of precisely this kind of thing happening. But it is only a possibility. There isn't at the moment a great deal of enthusiasm for the rather hybrid function of a deacon, so the whole experiment may fail. In that case all progress would be compromised. Should we wait to see how the married diaconate works out before making a decision about married priests? Not all slowness is wise. When it is a matter of governing communities, it is not always advisable to let situations get worse.

3

Worker-Priests and Professional Priests

THE NINETY specialists meeting in Lucerne during the summer of 1967 at a seminar of the Institute for Sacerdotal Assistance adopted a resolution saying that "the situation of the Church in different countries requires that certain priests and deacons exercise a secular profession on a full-time basis."

There is a growing desire to see priests adopt a secular profession. In an influential article Monsignor Illitch has proposed that married and professional laymen be ordained priests.[1] Missionaries living in Chili have expressed a similar wish. In countries as different as England and Spain priests have asked permission to seek secular employment.

This tendency is particularly strong among young priests (and better understood by young laymen). A survey of country priests in France asked: "Will worker-priests be necessary in the future?" Forty-eight percent of those in the twenty-five to thirty-three age bracket answered affirmatively (42 percent negatively) and only 38 percent in the thirty-four to forty-three age bracket, 34 percent in the forty-four to fifty-three age bracket, 25 percent in the fifty-four to sixty-three age bracket and 23 percent of those over sixty-four.[2]

There are objective arguments for such an innovation. In our civilization the exercise of a profession is necessary to human fulfillment. It matures us. In work man "is capable, even though dependent, of establishing his autonomy."[3] By realizing, he realizes himself. He finds an answer to the need of efficacy that is within him. It is a legitimate need, for this efficacy gives him a sense of his own worth. Moreover, the professional man is economically emancipated. He no longer has to depend on his family or, in the case of the priest, his community or diocese. "Money earned expresses and symbolizes a sucessful exchange, another's recognition of the value of our activity. It also enhances our autonomy and interior liberty. One has a feeling of participation rather than dependence."[4] Professional activity, moreover, enables one to become an integral member of society. Through it the

---

[1] Published in France by *Esprit,* October, 1967.
[2] Maître, *op. cit.*
[3] Maurice Merleau-Ponty, *Sense and Non-Sense,* tr. by Hubert L. and Patricia Allen Dreyfus (Evanston, Northwestern University Press, 1964).
[4] Marc Oraison, "Un homme sans métier," *Christus,* October, 1965.

individual shares in the realization of common projects, the transformation of nature and the pursuit of creation. This is so deep a human need that a man without a social function is practically ostracized.

The cleric had a social function in former times. He participated by reason of his priesthood in the life of the human community. But in secular society his role, a necessary one moreover, is not recognized. He is considered a more or less marginal figure.

There are two mutually complementary ways of reintegrating him into society, thus enabling him to achieve personal fulfillment: either the priest must adopt a secular profession or his sacerdotal function must be "professionalized."

A missionary urgency makes adoption of a secular profession necessary. The principal reason is not to bring the priest into contact with unbelievers or anyone else. Hours spent working on a machine, in a noisy shop, are not favorable to making contacts. Moreover, to consider work as a mere occasion of "contact," a pretext, would be to show little respect for an essential dimension of men's lives. One must truly assume it. Still, this desire for "contact" inspired the first worker-priests in France. Later, as their numbers diminished and theological reflection deepened, they were looked upon as a "sign" of the Church's interest in the workers and her desire to break down the wall that separated them. The priest-workers were also a means for the clerical society to get to know directly a world foreign to it.

But the import of what is suggested here is much more general. It is not merely a question of recouping lost prestige in those countries where the Church has lost it. It seems desirable that there be worker-priests everywhere, sharing more fully in the life of the community, in a common human existence.

Such participation would in itself justify secular work on the part of the priest. In addition, he would come to know the difficulties and hopes of others in a practical way and thus avoid that idealism which is his besetting fault, that nostalgia for a world he only imagines. Work would give him an immediate experience of the world. He would be center stage, ready to accept the audience's approval or disapproval with the rest of the actors, rather than a behind-the-scenes "prompter." Sharing their existence, he could better help Catholic laymen discover the Christian meaning of life and understand the unbeliever's point of view. As Teilhard de Chardin wrote: "To influence any walk of life effectively, we must be part of it. Only a worker can be understood by workers; only geologists and soldiers can speak to geologists and soldiers. Only a man will be listened to by other men." Perhaps men would find daily encounter with one who is like them, yet so different, disturbing. Be that as it may, there could no longer be any doubt about the Church's mission to the world. She would be totally immersed in the world through her priests as well as the laity. And, at the same time, the clerical society would disintegrate.

We need not ask ourselves if this kind of priest is possible in the Church, since he already exists: priest-workers, professors, journalists, editors, administrators who live like businessmen, pilgrimage directors who act like travel agents and many others. And there is no reason why the field should be restricted. The possibilities are limitless: doctors, military officers, painters, scientists, and so forth. All are equally desirable.

There are, however, various objections to priests engaging in secular work. Some people, for example, are afraid that such priests won't be so easy to handle, that they will constitute a new breed whose stock in trade will no longer be pious platitudes and inapplicable principles.

Let us consider some of these objections in more detail.

A first objection is one of principle. The priest, it is claimed, should be supported by the Church and do the Church's work. Yet St. Paul, often held up as an ideal for priests, was a tent maker. Priests in every century have imitated him in this.

Other objections are of a practical order. There are those who fear that priests exercising a profession would be second rate. This is not so true of the worker-priests who still enjoy a romantic aura that has by now become legendary. But what about a priest who works in an office? It would depend in the final analysis on his professional competence. It seems, on the basis of the cases we have studied, that priests in the secular world are much esteemed at all levels of public opinion if they are competent. Moreover, this esteem extends beyond his professional competence to the man as priest. Only the traditional clergy, whose way of life would be threatened, are contemptuous of priests in secular professions. Their contempt is indicated by the label "part-time priests," as though they were priests only while celebrating the liturgy.

Exceptional spiritual qualities will be required of such men. But we cannot assume that professional activity will automatically be dangerous for the spiritual life of priests. If that were so, what about the laity? There is no need to get overwrought about priests succumbing "to the spirit of the world." In 1890, after it was decided that seminarians would be liable to military training, the then cardinal of Reims expressed a similar fear: "These young men have been spared dangerous contacts with the world and are happily ignorant of the malice and perversity of men. Now they are suddenly confronted with those dangers and seductions of life that have the least relationship to their vocation." Such language makes us smile today. The fear that priests in secu-

lar professions "will succumb to the spirit of the world" will
probably make our grandchildren smile.

Such men, furthermore, will have to be exceptionally generous since their spare time will for the most part be spent
in the work of the ministry. But must we despair of finding
generous men among the people of God? A profession is no
more an easy solution for the priest than is marriage. However, it seems to conform to the necessities and possibilities
of our time. The witness of a professional priest, with a
family to feed and committed *for life* to the service of the
Church, would be impressive. This obviously does not mean
that professional activity will solve the missionary problem.
But it would be a partial solution and offer an answer to the
anguished questions of those priests who want "to rejoin
the human race."

The principal objection to professional engagement concerns the ministry: who would exercise it and how? This is
a serious objection but it must be qualified. As a professional,
the priest remains a priest and can exercise the ministry in
his professional capacity. Who, in the present situation, does
the parish priest meet when all the men and a good percentage of the women are at work? Children, old people,
those who are on vacation. Apart from funerals, sometimes
a marriage, and daily Mass for a few old women, what serious work can he do? Of course the modern priest is busy,
even overworked. But he is perhaps an unwitting victim of
Parkinson's law according to which work expands to fill the
time allotted to it.

On the other hand, many priests don't have enough to do.
Father David O'Neill offers this considered opinion:

"I know that it is a popular image of the Catholic priest
that he is hardworking and devoted, that his professional
work extends over long hours of unremitting toil. In the
judgment of a great number of priests with whom I have

talked, this is very generally not so, except in missionary areas of emerging countries. . . . My own experience in the priesthood has brought me into close working contact with members of many other professions, physicians, psychiatrists, social workers, psychologists, university lecturers and professors. I am convinced that, on the average, these members of the other professions dealing directly with human beings, their needs and problems, work more devotedly and for longer hours each week than does the average secular priest. . . . This view of the work-load of priests applies particularly in those areas in which priests are relatively plentiful. In many other places, the priest is kept very busy with his routine sacramental duties and with a bare minimum of personal teaching and instruction. However, in the well-developed areas, which have only between 400 to 1000 Catholics to each priest, these essential duties of the priest do not normally take up a very large proportion of his time." [5]

Without denying the diversity of situations, we must admit that the accusation of laziness, still made against priests by the people, is not without foundation. The nineteenth-century priest occupied himself with tasks that his successor today considers "unpriestly." But the latter has not in all cases found more acceptable substitutes. Much of his time is still taken up with marginal and even irrelevant duties. A better organization of the priest's work load would no doubt free him for more fruitful activities. Also, less bureaucracy, which is beginning to invade the Church at all levels, is greatly to be desired. Many of the administrative positions currently being held by priests could easily be taken over by laymen.

Priests are not alone in the Church and much of their work is not strictly ministerial. Professional laymen, nuns and brothers could be of great assistance in this respect. We

[5] *Op. cit.*, pp. 63–64.

already have a number of competent men and women teaching catechism, doing marriage counseling and even teaching theology. There is no reason why their numbers should not increase.

The concentration in the single person of the priest of all functions necessary to the Christian community is the result of the rural parochial system inherited from the Middle Ages. Today they can be shared by the laity. I don't think we need fear a lack of lay volunteers. Laymen are reluctant to give of their time primarily when they are assigned minor responsibilities. In a country like France, where the clergy considers itself rather enlightened, the laity are rarely given more than a material role in the parish. In this way the priest can continue to remain ignorant of the hard realities of the world. A more responsible division of labor, encouraged in part by the increasing numbers of priests in secular occupations, would perhaps put an end to the priest-layman dualism that has long plagued the Church and finally force priests to collaborate with the laity.

Thus the answer to the objection that the ministry would suffer if the priest engaged in profane work implies a complete reorganization of the Christian community. Moreover, such an answer cannot be fully convincing until this reorganization has begun. It will take a good deal of courage to attempt a reform of this magnitude. But we cannot escape the question: given the new image and role of the priest, how will the Church of tomorrow survive? It would be irresponsible not to try to answer it.

There can be no global answer since situations vary. We cannot imagine the same ecclesial structure for Asia and Africa as for urban, industrialized countries. In reaffirming episcopal collegiality the Council recognized the principle of national and regional differences. In what follows, I shall be speaking primarily about western countries where in about thirty years, according to sociologists, 90 percent of the population will be living in cities.

In the great urban complexes the individual is anonymous and alone in the crowd. He is also highly mobile and accustomed to traveling long distances. Under such circumstances, how can the people of God be assembled into veritable communities?

For some decades now the traditional parish has been a failure. In the rural world, parishes coincide rather exactly with a human community. The elements of social, economic and Christian life are in perfect harmony. But the huge urban parishes, numbering thousands of souls, can no longer fulfill their original aim, which was to bring the Church to all Christians. People in cities live in one area, work in another and have their social life in still another. A parish system that is still effective in the country is clearly incapable of functioning in the city.

Critics of the existing parish system often contradict themselves. Some find them too large. How can one form a community of 50,000 people? And even though practice has fallen off in the large city parish, priests still have all they can do in administering to those who still seek their services.

Others think that the urban parish is too small. It is limited to one section of the city and has no real concern for the city as a whole. It cannot contact those who work or socialize elsewhere. Because it is so restricted, the clergy are badly distributed. As a result the parish priest and his assistants are obliged to be polyvalent and occupy themselves with everything from administering the sacraments to instructing the repairman. "Perfect," say some. "He is thus all things to all men." They do not seem to realize that if he is a specialist in everything, he is condemned in an age of specialization to be competent in nothing.

Two Parisian priests, Francis Conan and Jean-Claude Bar-

reau, in their recent book *Demain la paroisse* offer a fresh
argument against those who think the parish is too small and
they propose some structural reforms. They point out that
almost every initiative in the French Church for the past
forty or fifty years has taken place outside of the parish—
priest-workers, Catholic Action, and so forth. This pattern
has gradually created a dangerous dualism: the parish on
the one hand and, on the other, priests and laymen carrying
out their Christian mission in the world. But this cannot be
tolerated because the parish must "manifest" the whole
Church. It must therefore synthesize the principal functions
of the Church. But in fact it does not do so. On the contrary,
everything is at sixes and sevens. In order to coordinate
extra-parochial and parochial activities there has been much
talk of a "total pastorate." But the bishop is too far away
and the intermediary authorities capable of directing such
an initiative are rare. Thus there has so far been more talk
than action.

What is to be done? A meeting ground must be found
where the pastor, the working priest, the school chaplain
and the responsible laymen can elaborate a common action.
Fathers Conan and Barreau propose that this meeting ground
might be the "englobing parish," a kind of super-parish that
would cover a vast territory and unite several of the present
parishes into large centers. Some efforts along these lines
have already been made.

The super-parish could be instrumental in regrouping the
Christian community. Laymen could meet there and "participate in the great pastoral initiatives of their local Church,
forming a veritable deliberating local assembly in union with
the clergy. This assembly might meet every year with the
clergy, the leaders of Christian movements and laymen
elected by the practicing communities all participating." The
priests of the super-parish, constituting with the pastor a

"presbyterium," could specialize in certain lines of work without letting their specialization isolate them from one another or from the parishes, as is the case today.

According to the authors of *Demain la paroisse,* these priests would engage in three kinds of activity:

1. Ministry to practicing communities of Christians, which would naturally be multiplied. To be fraternal such communities would have to be small. The larger Church could take care of such formal ceremonies as confirmation, solemn profession of faith and marriages.

2. Chaplaincies of all kinds. Efficiency would be stressed. Where formerly four chaplains worked with four small groups, one chaplain would work in a more organized fashion with a larger group.

3. One or several "missionary" teams made up of priests and laymen would be sent to unbelievers. They would take charge of those who are psychologically "distant" from the parish: workers, businessmen, young people and so forth.

The structure proposed by Fathers Conan and Barreau seems to respond to present needs. But it envisages no change in the priest's status. My proposals should, on the other hand, prove helpful in this respect.

Moreover, the authors aren't too clear about the size of these practicing communities. They seem to think that they should, at least in some cases, coincide with present parish boundaries. In that case the principal disadvantage of the present system is not solved. Real, human communities should be much smaller—at most a few families who are closely bound together either geographically or in some other way. Such communities, under the leadership of a priest, already exist in some countries, thus forming a kind of "underground Church."

A priest engaged in profane work seems eminently suited to lead small Christian communities in worship. He need not be married, for there is no necessary connection between profane work and marriage. Anyway, a single priest could work just as effectively with these small communities.[6] Such communities, more responsive than the anonymous masses who fill our churches today and adopting a different liturgy, would be much more attractive. Father Daniel O'Hanlon, S.J., has made a study of the Pentecostals, perhaps the fastest growing religious body in the world today, and concluded that the basic reason for their growth "is that when a forgotten human being comes to one of them, he feels himself loved and understood. One Puerto Rican Pentecostal compared the Catholic Church in this country to a supermarket —cold and formal."[7] Father O'Hanlon recommended that Catholics form ecclesial groups under the leadership of a priest and small enough to be real communities. But unless married men exercising a profane profession are admitted to the priesthood, it would be difficult if not impossible to find a sufficient number of ministers to lead these communities.

In addition to these smaller communities there should exist what have come to be known as "religious service stations"—the large brick churches that are our present parishes. There mobile, modern man could always find a priest, regular Masses and the sacraments. And, as we said, the larger Church could sponsor the more formal ceremonies.

These "religious service stations" obviously could not be staffed by priests engaged in profane work. They would have to be served by full-time priests (who might, of course, be married). Likewise, certain chaplaincies (hospitals, military, national lay movements, and so forth) would require permanent priests.

[6] Some, like Monsignor Illitch, propose that this kind of priest commit himself for a limited time rather than for life. This raises the question of the permanent character of the sacrament of orders.
[7] Daniel J. O'Hanlon, S.J., "The Pentecostals and Pope John's New Pentecost," *America*, May 4, 1963, p. 634.

If we grant the advantages of profane work for the priest, wouldn't the "permanent" priest, who is by definition excluded from this kind of activity, suffer the same disadvantages of the clergy today? There is a very real danger that he would. This might be avoided if priests were permanently engaged in neither the ministry nor profane work but had the opportunity (even the duty) to alternate between the two, depending on their desires and the needs of the Church. Moreover, some priests would no doubt be more attracted by permanent functions. Still, this would not be enough to offset the danger mentioned above.

What is needed to overcome the present disorder, amateurism and improvisations is a veritable "professionalization" of the priesthood. The ministry itself must be considered a profession. There is nothing dishonorable about this. In fact, trends in this direction are already apparent. For example, it was announced in November, 1966, that the priests of the archdiocese of Chicago had formed an association to defend their professional and social interests, although the association is not a union and recognizes episcopal authority.

But what more exactly, do we mean by professionalization?

First of all, a serious selection of candidates. All professions demand ability and competence. Speaking of ability, St. Paul wrote to Timothy: "Impose hands not lightly upon any man." Priests are still being ordained too young. Their maturity has not been tested, nor is their freedom of choice assured. The greatest number of departures are among those priests who were ordained young. The diaconate would be more meaningful if it became a probationary stage, lasting several years, for the priesthood. Then ordination would be the supreme consecration of a man who is as fulfilled as possible. It would also give the candidate more time to

choose between marriage and celibacy. In the present state
of affairs, that choice is made too soon. As Willibald Demal
points out, the psychic and biological characteristics of a
young man are substantially different from those of a mature
man. Many young people, he says, gladly accept the priesthood but suffer enormously in later life because of the burden of celibacy and would gladly renounce their first decision if it were still possible.[8]

To guarantee professional competence, the present system
of formation will have to be radically overhauled. Why
should men who are to live and work in the world be shut
up in specialized institutions? A happy evolution is discernible in many seminaries, which the 1967 Synod should accelerate. Seminaries will have to open their doors and enlist
the collaboration of lay men and women as well as priests
in the active ministry. Furthermore, seminarians should
ideally engage in profane activities. In Holland, the fifty
major seminaries and religious novitiates that were scattered
through the country were replaced with five "schools of
theology," all of which are located in large urban centers.
Many of their students live in apartments or rooming houses.
It is also desirable that these "open" seminaries be located
near universities so that future priests can mingle with the
students.

But other reforms will be necessary in the case of those
who are to be ordained after the age of thirty. They should,
as a general rule, have some profane competence in order to
be able to choose, depending upon their aspirations, between
the permanent ministry and secular activity. At the basis of
all of these reforms should be the principle that continuing
formation is more important than a limited, preliminary

[8] Cf. Willibald Demal, *Pastoral Psychology in Practice* (Cork, Ireland,
Mercier Press).

formation. Recent initiatives in this direction are hopefully the sign of things to come.

As for the contents of this formation, I would express two hopes. First, that all priests receive a philosophical and theological formation that is both sound and adapted to the needs of men today. Those destined for the permanent ministry should receive a solid professional training for the pastorate, including the study of psychology and sociology. Secondly, not all priests should receive the same formation. If we recognize different kinds of priests, we ought to provide different kinds of formation.

The second mark of professionalism is specialization. Until now, priests have taken on the whole episcopal function, with the exception of ordaining and confirming. But circumstances have created a much greater degree of pluralism. Some priests devote themselves to the work of evangelization; others specialize in bringing the Word to unbelievers; others become catechetical experts; and others distribute the sacraments, and so forth. Specialization is a law of life.

And it must be accepted realistically. We are still too inclined to think that the priest must be polyvalent. Some priests will be excellent teachers although they will fail pitifully with adults. Others are at home with workers but would be frustrated in a rural assignment. Others, finally, would be bored in a parish but could work wonders in Catholic Action. Polyvalence is necessarily amateurish. Specialization develops and supposes competence. Many young people, moreover, would be more attracted to the priesthood if they knew they could work in the field they are most suited for. In the present system, many aspirants to the priesthood are rejected if they insist on specializing.

Specialization would force a total revision of the system of nominations. More attention would be given to the specialties and interests of each individual. Despite the real and recent efforts of many bishops, it is still true to say that few private enterprises treat their personnel as offhandedly as does the Church. A priest should never be assigned to a position unless he has been previously consulted. His objections ought to be listened to. There should be established procedures of recourse in case of abuses, as in civil society. Other procedures should also be studied to permit laymen and other priests to have a voice in nominations, at least in some cases.

A third characteristic of professionalism is remuneration. The permanent priest should be salaried by the Christian community and not by the state. His personal revenue and expenses should be distinguished from those of the Christian community. A few simple rules would assure the application of this principle. Priests could be paid by the diocese and their salaries standardized. A salary scale ought to be established for permanent priests, working priests (who would be paid by their employers), and married priests. The permanent priest, moreover, should be compensated for his professional expenses (travel, educational materials, etc.). The necessary resources would be more readily donated by the Christian laity if they were convinced that they were being seriously managed and if all accounts were made public.

The priest would gain in security. He would also become more realistic since he would be responsible for his own budget and assured a dignified way of life. Being salaried, he would share in the common experience of the majority of men today.

If such reforms were introduced, one of the least admitted causes of the uneasiness of priests would perhaps disappear. They would no longer be ashamed of their poverty. They could, finally, enjoy the respect it merits without suffering the suspicions that it provokes.

Specialized professional priests, working in all sectors of human activity, might well be a cause of concern.[9] Wouldn't such diversity be a prelude to disintegration? The disintegration of the clergy is no cause for concern. It is devoutly to be wished for. The unity of the priesthood would be preserved in the con-celebration of the Mass which the Council restored to a place of honor. The necessary unifying role must be carried out by an institution—the presbyterium— and by a man—the bishop. Wouldn't the presbyterium be much more meaningful if it included different types of priests? And the bishop's role would itself be profoundly affected. More bishops would undoubtedly be necessary in order to establish closer contact with priests. Nor can the choice of a bishop any longer be left up to a nuncio, who very often has newly arrived from Rome and is unfamiliar with the real issues of the country he has been named to. Priests, laymen and, more directly today, episcopal conferences of the interested countries should have an important say in this matter.[10]

To question the situation of priests is at the same time to question the whole pastoral organization of the Church. That is perhaps why we are reluctant to confront the problem and openly propose solutions that may be revolutionary yet safeguard the nature of the priesthood. These "structural" solu-

[9] To complete this picture of diversity, we should mention the many religious orders, although this book is not directly concerned with their problems. We might note in passing that those who belong to recently created orders have problems that are rather similar to those of the secular clergy.
[10] Hans Küng and others suggest that bishops be nominated for a limited period of time like religious superiors. On this view, nomination for life is no longer adapted to our age (interview, March 19, 1967, on Radio Luxembourg). The trend is in this direction: retirement of aged bishops, more frequent changes of dioceses, and so forth.

tions are by no means the only ones necessary. A renewal of clerical spirituality, among other things, is certainly desirable. But structural changes can bring about others.

The proposals I have made are for the most part not original. In the intense ferment of the present almost all of them have been suggested, although frequently in quasi-secrecy. It is my opinion that the time has come to put our cards on the table, to discuss our problems in the clear light of day. If we expect the meaning of the Church to be strengthened among priests and laymen, the problems of the Church must be openly debated by an informed public opinion. If this were the case and if the Church dared take the means necessary to destroy the clerical society, she would no doubt be able to communicate the faith itself to those men and women of goodwill who believe in Christ but are turned away by His Body which is the Church.

I have made my own opinions and preferences clear throughout the book. This may be presumptuous. But it would be dishonest to act like a spectator when one is an actor.

The proposals here advanced are like "target boats," as the sailors say. They are offered for what they are worth. Others may have different suggestions concerning the de-clericalization of the priesthood and the abolition of the clerical society. But if this book contributes to the debate, it will have served its purpose. Moreover, the desirability of abolishing the clerical society for the great good of all—priests and laymen of today and tomorrow—in order to increase the Church's influence does not seem to be any longer a subject of discussion. It is time for action. If we do not mercifully intervene, the clerical society will die of sclerosis and anemia. It is already in its death throes. Its demise may seriously hurt the Church. It may. But the worst, happily, is not always inevitable.